HOW TO HA...

HEALING MINISTRY

IN ANY CHURCH

A COMPREHENSIVE GUIDE

*How the Holy Spirit Is Moving in Today's
Traditional, Evangelical Churches*

*How Your Church Can Carry on the
Healing Works of Jesus*

*Why Spiritual Reawakening Is Happening
in the Hearts of People Worldwide*

C. PETER WAGNER

Regal Books

A Division of Gospel Light
Ventura, California, U.S.A.

Published by Regal Books
A Division of Gospel Light
Ventura, California 93006
Printed in U.S.A.

Library of Congress Catalog in Publication Data

Wagner, C. Peter.
    How to have a healing ministry without making your church sick.

    Includes index.
    1. Spiritual healing. 2. Church work with the sick. I. Title.
BT732.5.W324   1988   234'.13   88-18493
ISBN 0-8307-1297-6

Rights for publishing this book in other languages are contracted by
Gospel Literature International (GLINT). GLINT also provides technical
help for the adaptation, translation, and publishing of Bible study
resources and books in scores of languages worldwide. For further
information, contact GLINT, Post Office Box 488, Rosemead, California, 91770, U.S.A., or the publisher.

4 5 6 7 8 9 10 11 12 / 96 95 94 93 92

Dedicated to

THE SCHALLER FAMILY
Michael and Cathy
Gabriel, Rebekah and Rachael

CONTENTS

From the Author

When many people first see or hear the title of this book, they respond with a simultaneous nod and chuckle. The nod is an affirmation that having a healing ministry in their church wouldn't be a bad idea. The chuckle is really a nervous laugh, nervous because they're not sure it could happen without making their church sick.

Reasons for this are not obscure. Throughout the twentieth century the most prominent new feature to appear on the Christian landscape worldwide has been the Pentecostal/charismatic movement, and reactions to it on the part of the more traditional forms of mainline Christianity have been varied. Some, particularly in the early part of the century, considered the Pentecostals a cult. Later they gained a measure of respectability, but many still preferred to keep Pentecostals at arm's length because of a certain residual attitude of disdain for "those tongue speakers" or "Holy Rollers" or "that hillbilly religion." When the charismatic movement appeared more recently, denominations and local churches felt the affect of new tensions, resulting at times in painful splits.

In the closing years of this century, however, we see a different picture. Nevertheless, many evangelical Christians across the board have decided that, while they recognize a significant work of God in the Pentecostal and charismatic movements, they prefer to remain outside those movements. And any attempt to coerce them to become even closet charismatics is resisted.

At the same time, it is impossible for any active observer of God's work in the world today not to acknowledge that there is a certain vitality, an excitement about God, a spiritual energy among Pentecostals and charismatics that we wish we could see more of in our own churches. While we may not want to join them, we feel a bit of justifiable envy, and say, "God, can't we experience some of that power also?" Many of us, for example, would like to see our more traditional churches have an overt, powerful and effective ministry of healing. So many people are hurting physically, emotionally and spiritually, and we would like to help them in tangible ways, more than we have so far been able to do. Seeing this power operate is so much like the New Testament. It is so much like Jesus.

If you find yourself identifying with these feelings, this book will be good news for you, because I believe it can be done.

I describe the Pentecostal movement as the first wave of the powerful movement of God's spirit in the twentieth century, the charismatic movement as the second wave, and then I see a third wave in which the Holy Spirit is manifesting the same kind of power in our traditional evangelical churches that we have seen in the first two waves, without requiring us to abandon our particular distinctives or traditions. In other words, without making our churches or denominations sick.

Some may wonder whether a book like this is not just some attractive bait designed to hook them into the Pentecostal or charismatic movements. I hope you don't see it that way. If it makes you appreciate all the more what God has been doing through the first two waves in recent decades, I will rejoice. If it opens your mind to learn things God has to teach us through the Pentecostal and charismatic movements, then we'll all be greatly enriched.

A large amount of what I share as third-wave teaching was first learned through the first and second waves. But I am not, nor do I ever intend to be, a Pentecostal or a charismatic. For 16 years I have been a member of Lake Avenue Congregational Church in Pasadena, California and I hope to remain a member for at least 16 more.

While I am addressing this book primarily to traditional evangelicals such as those I fellowship with in my church, I also hope God will use it to encourage members of the first two waves. I don't think I am telling family secrets to mention that some churches that once experienced great power in healing have not been seeing it to any degree for some time now. Theologically, the framework for healing has been laid, it is preached from the pulpit, but the experience is minimal.

My prayer is that God will use this book to fan some Pentecostal and charismatic flames, which have died down, into a new baptism with the fire of the Holy Spirit. If it happens, I see the three waves, together under one King of kings and Lord of lords moving into the greatest and most exciting period of the expansion of the kingdom of God history has ever known.

C. Peter Wagner
Pasadena, California
1988

ONE

THE THIRD WAVE

housands of Christians are now exclaiming, This is a new day for the Church!

I happen to believe they are right. Admittedly, across 2000 years of Christian history, it is not the first time new days have dawned. Roman Christians might have said it was a new day when Constantine took the throne. Iberian Christians might have said it when Columbus returned with stories of the New World. German Christians might have said it when Luther appeared before the Diet of Worms. But none of them could have been more excited than today's Christian leaders who have the ability to discern God's hand moving throughout our contemporary world.

For one thing, the harvest has never been more ripe. Currently, by conservative estimates, each day sees

78,000 new Christians. While many of these are born into families of what some would classify as nominal Christians (Christians in name only), nevertheless, a conservative estimate of 14,000 come as adult conversions.[1] Conservative, because the figure might actually be twice that high.

Explosive church growth is occurring in numerous countries of the world, such as China where over 50 million practicing Christians are now reported, or Korea where numerous local churches count their membership in tens of thousands, or Argentina where up to 8,000 decisions for Christ are reported each day (although only a small proportion of them can be accommodated in the already overflowing churches). Even more significantly, during the twentieth century the percentage of Christians as compared to the total world population has been increasing.

In America, receptivity to the gospel is high. While many of the traditional mainline denominations have been losing members, the loss is more than made up by the vigorous growth of evangelical churches and denominations including Pentecostals and charismatics. At least six sanctuaries seating 10,000 or more have been constructed in the last eight years with more than that number to be added in the next eight. A number of new church starts have mushroomed to several thousand members in less than five years, many of them pastored by young people in their 30s. One U.S. church has announced its goal of 100,000 members.

Not only has the harvest never been more ripe, but the harvesters have never been as well-equipped as they are today. Significant research is clarifying the global task as never before. Think tanks such as the U.S. Center for World Mission, World Vision's MARC (Mission

Advance Research and Communication Center), the Southern Baptist Foreign Mission Board, the Lausanne Committee for World Evangelization, schools of world mission at leading evangelical seminaries and many others are producing the kind of task-oriented information that accelerates the completion of the Great Commission.

The fields of missiology, evangelism, cross-cultural communication and church growth are expanding rapidly. Seminary and Bible college graduates are equipped with skills virtually unheard of a generation ago. Whereas most missionaries traditionally have been sent out by Western churches, over 20,000 from Third World churches have now joined them in ministry across the globe. The doldrums of the '60s when churches were disparaged and evangelism was scorned and God was declared dead have now given way to a new sunrise in the transition years from the twentieth to the twenty-first centuries.

Yes, it is a new day for the Church.

NEW SPIRITUAL POWER

A major reason for the dawning of a new day has been an unprecedented release of spiritual power through the Pentecostal and charismatic movements, both emerging and flowering in the twentieth century.

My field of research, writing and teaching is church growth. Since I was trained by Donald McGavran at Fuller Seminary in the late '60s, I have been vitally interested in knowing where churches are experiencing God's blessing in growth, and why. When I began my work with McGavran I was anti-Pentecostal. While I might grudgingly have admitted that Pentcostals may be Christians, I suspected they were not the kind of Christians that pleased God very much. But McGavran taught me that the Body of Christ was broader than I had believed and that God loved the entire Body. Furthermore, he helped me to develop "church growth eyes" through which I began to see and appreciate the work of the Holy Spirit in bringing men and women to the Father regardless of the denominational label they might carry.

At that time I was a missionary to Bolivia. When I returned to the field, the first thing my new church growth eyes saw was the startling but irrefutable fact that throughout Latin America the growth of the Pentecostal churches was far outstripping that of all the other Christian traditions put together, including mine. I immediately began to research Pentecostal church growth, I found my enthusiasm growing, and I published a book on it in the early '70s called *Look Out! The Pentecostals are Coming.* I have recently rewritten and updated it under the title, *Spiritual Power and Church Growth.*[2]

What is true about the growth of Pentecostal churches in Latin America is also true of what we now call the Pentecostal/charismatic movement in most parts of the world today. When we look at the total picture, research shows that there is substantial church growth in some places without supernatural signs and wonders. There are also many instances of rather amazing healings and miracles and deliverances with little or no church growth following. But, across the board, on a wide scale, the most vigorous growth of Christian churches is accompanied by the characteristic signs and wonders of the Pentecostal/charismatic movement.

I will provide some statistics and illustrations later on in the book.

What is the anatomy of this new spiritual power? Is it the exclusive property of Pentecostals and charismatics, or is it available to other Christians as well? These, and other similar questions, are being asked by thoughtful Christians in this new day of the Church.

IS THERE A THIRD WAVE?

My friend Michael Cassidy of African Enterprise thinks of himself as one of those who "live in that theological twilight between a rather rigid evangelicalism and a full-blown Pentecostalism." In *Bursting the Wineskins* he speaks of people who are aware of this new spiritual power that I have described and who wish to see it operate in their ministries, but for various reasons do not feel free to identify with the contemporary charismatic renewal movement.[3]

During the decade of the '80s a significantly increasing number of traditional evangelicals ... have been seeking and finding a new spiritual power.

I know exactly where Michael is coming from. because I find myself in the same position. And we are not alone. Especially during the decade of the '80s a significantly increasing number of traditional evangelicals, as well as some who might prefer to position themselves slightly to the left of evangelicalism, have been seeking and finding a new spiritual power. Anglican

Canon James Wong of Singapore sees the new trend clearly. "I would call it the new wave of the Holy Spirit," he says. "I don't even see it as a charismatic force," he adds. "I see it as a tremendous revival and awakening of spiritual hunger in the hearts of people when they see the Holy Spirit working sovereignly with signs and wonders."[4]

This picture of the never-never land between a dispensationally-oriented evangelicalism and Pentecostalism began to come clear in the early '80s. As I was wrestling with my own identity with what the Holy Spirit seemed to be doing, I was interviewed by Kevin Perrotta of *Pastoral Renewal* magazine in 1983. Toward the end of a rather thorough discussion, he asked me a perceptive question. He asked if what I was describing was really something new or if it was actually part of what we have seen in the Pentecostal and charismatic movements. For the first time that I can recall I used the expression *third wave*, as I responded to his question.[5]

I went on to explain that I do see it as something new. I believe that in the twentieth century we have been witnessing the most powerful outpouring of the Holy Spirit on the world Church that history has ever known. At least in magnitude, if not also in quality, it surpasses even the first century. The first wave of this outpouring was the initiation and development of the Pentecostal movement in the very beginning of the century. The second wave was the charismatic movement, which started around 1960. Both of these waves have seen, and I believe will continue to see, explosive church growth. The hand of God is upon them in an extraordinary way.

The third wave, which began to take on a self-identity in the U.S. around 1980, enfolds the people

Michael Cassidy and James Wong have identified. When I casually used the term *third wave* in 1983, I had no idea if it would stick. We in the church growth movement have learned through experience that perhaps one out of five neologisms ever proves to be useful to anyone other than the person coining the term. But since Kevin Perrotta chose to use it in the title of the article, which was quoted and reprinted in several other places, I decided to continue to identify myself publicly as a member of this third wave.

Only history will show if the term is acceptable. To date two recognized researchers, one from the first wave and one from the second, have begun to use the term. Vinson Synan, a classical Pentecostal who has gained the well-deserved reputation as a chief historian of the movement, includes a section on the third wave in his recent book *In the Latter Days*. He observes: "By the mid 1980s there was evidence that the 'third wave' was indeed entering the mainline churches without the confusion of labels that had caused such great problems in the past."[6]

And David Barrett, the charismatic Anglican who is renowned as the editor of the *World Christian Encyclopedia*, has recently been concentrating his energies on researching the Pentecostal/ charismatic movements. In his latest statistical tables he has added a section labeled third wave. In private conversation he admitted that when he first heard the term several years ago he didn't like it, but upon further reflection he now feels it to be an accurate label for a discrete group. He counts 27 million worldwide third-wavers in 1987, and lists as many as 50,000 back in 1970.[7]

Time will tell, but meanwhile I continue to argue that, yes, there is such a thing as a third wave.

PENTECOSTALS

If there is a third wave, it is important to know in some detail not only what it is, but also what it is not. As we have seen, those who identify with the third wave have chosen not to identify with the Pentecostal or charismatic movements. This choice should by no means be interpreted as an implicit criticism of either of the first two waves. I do not believe that any one of the waves is right while the other two are wrong. All three are committed to one Body, one Spirit, one hope, one Lord, one faith, one baptism and one God and Father of all (see Eph. 4:4-6). All hold a high view of the authority of Scripture and believe in the urgency of world evangelization. All are convinced that the power of God described in the Gospels and Acts is in effect as God's kingdom is manifested around the world today. The similarities are much greater than the differences. But there are important differences, for each group feels that God has chosen to minister through them in a particular way.

The Pentecostals came first. Historians trace the origin of the movement to either January 1, 1901 when students in Charles Parham's Bethel Bible School in Topeka, Kansas began speaking in tongues or to the famous Los Angeles Azusa Street revival led by William J. Seymour from 1906 to 1909, or to both. Through the years the major doctrine that has distinguished Pentecostals from other born-again, Bible-believing evangelicals is their doctrine of the "baptism in the Holy Spirit" as a work of grace distinct from the "new birth" accompanied by speaking in other tongues as the initial physical evidence. Other evangelicals, particularly of the Wesleyan holiness persuasion agree that there is a second work of grace, but see personal sanctification rather than tongues as the chief validation of the experience. For example, the major distinctive message of the man known as *Mr. Pentecost*, David du Plessis, had to do with "Jesus the baptizer."

I had the privilege of associating with David du Plessis during the final years of his life when he moved to Fuller Seminary (where I teach) in order to establish the David du Plessis Center for Christian Spirituality. He frequently told of his extensive 50-year ministry of building bridges between Pentecostals and other Christian churches, both Catholic and Protestant. Almost invariably he described the heart of his ministry as sharing the news that Jesus Christ, the Head of the Church, was the baptizer and that His baptism was in the Holy Spirit. He described speaking in other tongues as a consequence of the baptism in the Holy Spirit. Following that would come the fruit of the Holy Spirit in the life of the believer and ministry with the gifts of the Spirit.

When I first began to interact with Du Plessis I was in the beginning stages of witnessing signs and wonders in my own ministry and in the ministry of others close to me. I clearly recall that when I shared with some enthusiasm what I had been seeing his reaction was something akin to boredom. In fact, he offered some fatherly warnings about getting too excited about this. I discovered that in his own personal ministry, praying for the sick, casting out demons and expecting miracles were present, but they had assumed a comparatively low profile. Compared, that is, with the baptism in the Holy Spirit.

Since I was talking to *Mr. Pentecost*, I assumed that his point of view might be more than just personal, but representative of the movement. It was further reinforced by a statement from Thomas F. Zimmerman who, as President of the World Pentecostal Conference for many years, rivals Du Plessis as the top Pentecostal leader. A few years ago, Zimmerman was invited by *Christianity Today* to set forth his interpretation of "what is right in Pentecostalism." He summarizes his thoughts under six major headings. One of them explains the distinctive message of Pentecostals as "the baptism in the Holy Spirit with speaking in tongues." But I was surprised to find that none of the six points highlights an overt ministry of healing the sick and casting out demons (although prayers for the sick are mentioned in passing under the section on worship).[8]

Together with the doctrine of the baptism in the Holy Spirit as evidenced by speaking in other tongues, the classical Pentecostal movement developed a code of Christian conduct almost identical to that of fundamentalist Protestants, prevalent especially through the American Bible Belt. It became important to them to demonstrate their separation from the world through abstinence from such things as alcoholic beverages, smoking, dancing, card playing, movies, expletives in speech, and in some instances jewelry, makeup and professional coiffures.

CHARISMATICS

The second wave, the charismatics, date their beginning to April 1960 when Father Dennis Bennett, rector of St. Mark's Episcopal Church in Van Nuys, California shared publicly with his congregation that five months previously he had spoken in tongues as he prayed in the home of some friends. Precursors of the movement in Europe have been traced to 1950, and even to as early as 1910.

As the charismatic movement spread rapidly throughout the U.S. in the 1960s and '70s, it took the form of charismatic renewal groups within established denominations including Episcopalian, Methodist, Lutheran, Catholic, Baptist, Church of Christ, Mennonite, Orthodox, Presbyterian, United Church of Christ and others. Then, in the 1970s a new and extremely important phenomenon began to develop, namely the appearance of free-standing, independent charismatic congregations and clusters or fellowships of congregations, which function as minidenominations. In fact, by the 1980s this independent charismatic church movement had become one of the fastest growing segments of American religion.

The chief doctrinal distinctive of the charismatic movement is similar to that of the Pentecostal movement. One of its widely recognized leaders, Larry Christenson, Director of the International Lutheran Renewal Center, puts it this way: "A distinguishing mark of the charismatic renewal has been a wide-spread and distinctive experience which initially focuses upon the person and gifts of the Holy Spirit. The term most commonly used to designate this experience is "baptism with the Holy Spirit."[9]

As with the Pentecostals, the experience of baptism in the Holy Spirit as distinct from conversion is a key teaching of charismatics. However, their view of tongues as the initial physical evidence of the baptism is not as tight. Still, Christenson affirms that tongues has played a significant role in the development of the movement. "Without the emphasis on tongues," he says, "it is doubtful that there would have been either a Pentecostal or charismatic movement."[10]

Nevertheless, when pressed, an increasing number

of charismatic renewal leaders will admit that some Spirit-filled Christians, as they call those who have received "the baptism," may never have spoken in tongues. Deep down, however, almost all of them would argue that while tongues might not be indispensable, things usually go better with tongues.

While the doctrinal differences between Pentecostals and charismatics appear to outside observers to be slight, the differences in Christian life-style are often more obvious, and, in fact, have been the cause of a bit of intentional distancing on the part of Pentecostals from some charismatic brothers and sisters. For many Lutheran, Presbyterian, Episcopal, Catholic and United Church charismatics, taboos on alcoholic beverages, smoking, movies, dancing and the lot have little relationship to Christian sanctification. This has caused no small problem to some Pentecostal preachers who for years have preached against drinking beer or wine with the same fervor used in denouncing adultery, homosexuality, stealing or lying. Going out for a beer after a tongues-speaking renewal meeting just doesn't seem to compute to Pentecostals. Going out for pie a la mode is much more manageable.

It is fair to say that the codes of conduct in the newer independent charismatic church movement are closer to those of the Pentecostals than are the codes of conduct in denominational renewal movements. But a different point of tension has arisen here. Unlike the renewal groups, many independent charismatics are aggressively multiplying new churches and in some cases new functional denominations. To outsiders they look very much like Pentecostal churches, although subtle differences in worship style and ministry have been noticed by insiders. Some Pentecostals interpret this as ominous turf encroachment. At best they have been regarded with a we-they attitude by Pentecostal leaders. At worst they have been accused of "sheep stealing."

THE THIRD WAVE

How does the third wave differ from the Pentecostal and charismatic movements?

For emphasis, I repeat what I said before: The similarities are much greater than the differences. However, the differences are not unimportant, and I am going to attempt to spell them out.

Let me say at the outset that I speak only as an individual. I am not the President of the World Third Wave Conference—no such entity exists. I am only one of many leaders whom God seems to be raising up around the world to minister in a third-wave style. Exactly how many there are I do not yet know, but if David Barrett's estimate of 27 million believers associated with the third wave is anywhere near accurate, there must be a large number of them. The movement is in its incipient stages and clearer definitions will come into focus as time goes on. With that disclaimer I can move on to express the way I see the third wave at the moment.

As I analyze the distinctives of the third wave, three areas stand out: doctrinal, ecclesiastical and experiential.

1. Doctrinal Distinctives

Among Bible-believing evangelicals, doctrinal differences are acceptable on what, by consensus, are secondary issues. Baptism is an example. Methodists sprinkle, Baptists immerse and Quakers "dry clean." Each is firmly convinced they are doing it in the right way, but they generally tolerate the others. Most people these days don't consider it worth fighting over.

The very nature of theology itself allows for such differences. Theology is nothing more or less than a human attempt to explain God's Word and works in a reasonable and systematic way. The two principal sources of data are the Bible and Christian experience. It goes without saying that different people see the Bible in different ways and they interpret experience in different ways. And because there is disagreement, it doesn't mean that one point of view is necessarily wrong. They might well both be right, with each one emphasizing important facets of God's truth.

The major doctrinal issues separating the third wave from the first two waves involve some of these secondary doctrines, specifically the baptism in the Holy Spirit, tongues and spiritual gifts. Both points of view accept the Bible as their ultimate authority. And both have observed the same Christian experiences. For example, (a) Some Christians, subsequent to the new birth, experience a profound energizing of the Holy Spirit in their lives, and for some it occurs more than once; (b) Some Christians speak in tongues and some do not; (c) Sometimes (a) and (b) are parts of the same experience, but sometimes not. So how do we explain what the Bible teaches and what we learn from Christian experience?

As we have seen, most Pentecostals and charismatics call that experience baptism in the Holy Spirit and teach that you can tell if it has really happened to you by whether or not you have spoken in other tongues. They back it up by tying in Jesus words, "You shall be baptized with the Holy Spirit not many days from now" (Acts 1:5) with Pentecost where the 120 in the upper room "were all filled with the Holy Spirit and began to speak with other tongues" (2:4). This is a reasonable and systematic explanation of the data.

I believe that being filled with the Holy Spirit is . . . something Christians should expect to be repeated from time to time throughout their Christian lives.

While admitting this, I happen to believe that my way of understanding the data is even more reasonable and systematic than theirs. Here are my points in an abbreviated form:

My first observation is that this phenomenon of Christians being energized by the Holy Spirit is referred to as *filling* more than as *baptism* in the New Testament. In fact, the biblical account of the Pentecost experience itself does not say that the believers were "baptized in the Spirit" but rather that they were "filled with the Spirit" (2:4). I understand the introduction of the gospel to the Jews (see Acts 2), to the Samaritans (see Acts 8) and to the Gentiles (see Acts 10) as three phases of the total "Pentecostal event," which happened historically once for all. Subsequent to that, believers still needed to be filled with the Holy Spirit. Presumably some, if not most, of the group described in Acts 4:30 had been present at Pentecost. For sure Peter and John had. But "they were all filled with the Holy Spirit" once again on that occasion. Other biblical examples could be given.

I believe that being filled with the Holy Spirit is something that is not limited to a once-for-all experience (as is the new birth), but rather it is something Christians should expect to be repeated from time to time throughout their Christian lives.

My second observation is that the baptism of the Holy Spirit is truly enough a once-for-all experience and that it happens when we are born again. First Corinthians 12:13 says, "For by one Spirit we were all baptized into one body." I realize that David du Plessis would say that here the Holy Spirit is the baptizer but that we should also seek a second experience with Jesus as the baptizer. That is our difference.

My third observation is that speaking in tongues is a spiritual gift. It is just one of 27 different spiritual gifts that I believe God distributes throughout the Body of Christ "to each one individually as He wills" (1 Cor. 12:11). Some have the gift of tongues and some do not, just as some have the gifts of evangelist, hospitality or teacher and some do not.

My fourth observation is that one can be filled with the Holy Spirit and exhibit the fruit of the Spirit and minister through spiritual gifts in power and be a channel for healing the sick and casting out demons, all without speaking in tongues. After all, the apostle Paul raises the question: "Do all speak with tongues?" (1 Cor. 12:30). The obvious answer is no.

Therefore in the third wave you will not find people encouraging other Christians to seek the baptism in the Holy Spirit and you will not find tongues highlighted above any other gift.

Related to this is the doctrine of spiritual gifts. Many

Pentecostals and charismatics tend to emphasize the nine gifts in 1 Corinthians 12:8-10, regarding them as somewhat more indicative of Spirit-filled ministry than the other 18 gifts. Added to that is the notion that believers, when baptized in the Holy Spirit (as Pentecostals or charismatics understand it), gain potential access to all nine gifts throughout their Christian life. The third wave, as I will explain in due course, takes a different view on those issues, which, I again emphasize, are secondary doctrines.

2. Ecclesiastical distinctives

A chief characteristic of the third wave is to avoid divisiveness at almost any cost. The core of the third wave is composed of evangelical believers who are satisfied with their present ecclesiastical affiliation and desire that it remain intact.

One of the reasons why some evangelicals have decided they do not want to be identified with either the Pentecostal or charismatic movements is that these movements both have gained a reputation for divisiveness. For some, this is a bad rap, but in many cases it is deserved. The early Pentecostals, for example, emerged largely from the holiness movement. Although it was not their original intention or desire, they broke away and formed their own denominations following in the pathway of Luther and Wesley. The Church of the Nazarene, to cite one case, originally was called the Pentecostal Church of the Nazarene. But they reacted so strongly against what they considered an unbiblical emphasis on tongues among Pentecostals that they were forced to drop that part of their name, and three generations later they are still smarting. The charismatic renewal movement left a prominent trail of split churches throughout the 1960s and '70s.

In the decade of the '80s, divisiveness is much less of an issue, for which we are all thankful. But religious memories are long, and the fear that history might repeat itself lingers in many places.

Third-wave leaders are willing to compromise at many points in order not to disturb the philosophy of ministry of a traditional evangelical congregation. I find myself compromising constantly as I seek to minister at Lake Avenue Congregational Church, in Fuller Theological Seminary and in seminars sponsored by the Charles E. Fuller Institute for Evangelism and Church Growth. And I do so gladly because I feel that such is God's current calling on my life. But many of my contemporaries find they can't do this because they feel God is calling them in a different way. Some of them now pastor independent churches where they can do virtually everything they want to do the way they want to do it. In my opinion, they are where God wants them to be and I am where God wants me to be. They are in the second wave; I am in the third.

One of the areas of compromise I consider important in my particular context has to do with public tongues. A chief area of my ministry, as I will describe in more detail later on, is my Sunday School class in Lake Avenue Congregational Church called the 120 Fellowship. It is a third-wave group of around 100 adults. Early on, when many of the spiritual gifts were becoming evident in the class, I dealt with public tongues by categorically forbidding their use. I did this for two reasons. The first was that I knew enough about the history of charismatic divisiveness to realize that public tongues have been one of the most divisive elements. (Problems with tongues actually go back to the Corinthian church.) My desire for unity in the Body supersedes my desire to see all the gifts manifested.

Second, I wanted to agree with my senior pastor, Paul Cedar. In a private consultation he had encouraged me not to allow the public use of tongues in the class. He stated that several of his charismatic friends had taken the same position. However, he encouraged me to be led by the Holy Spirit. His rule for church functions was no public tongues. I felt it would be unwise for me to allow the class to take a different direction on such a potentially explosive matter.

When I told the class what our rule was, some came to me and said, Aren't you afraid of quenching the Holy Spirit? My reply was yes; I do have reservations in that area since the Bible says "do not forbid to speak with tongues" (1 Cor. 14:39). But it is a risk I am willing to take because the next verse says, "Let all things be done decently and in order" (v. 40). Furthermore, if the Spirit is quenched, I take full responsibility. God will not blame you personally if you refrain from using public tongues in obedience of those who are over you in the Lord. A greater spiritual risk for you is not to obey. Whether we have lost any class members on that score alone, I do not know. I suspect we may have lost one or two at the most.

A final point relating to ecclesiastical matters is semantic. One of the major causes of divisiveness has been the unintentional creation of categories of first-class Christians and second-class Christians within the same congregation. Although the best of the charismatics vigorously attempt to deny it, there is hardly any way of avoiding the impression that those who have received the "experience" have taken an important step to a higher plane of spirituality than they were on before. And, in sincere Christian love, they can do none other than reach back and attempt to help their brothers and sisters in Christ to take the same step.

The most common term used to describe this new spiritual status is the adjective *Spirit-filled*. The term is so common that many people do not realize how divisive it can be. It is not divisive, of course, in a Pentecostal or charismatic church where seeking the baptism in the Holy Spirit is an integral part of the philosophy of ministry. But it can easily be in an evangelical church where large numbers of mature Christians who walk closely with God can be made to feel second-class because they neither speak in tongues nor like to be around those who do. To see how pervasive this term is, check out how many times it is used in the average hour on a Christian television talk show. We hear of Spirit-filled churches and Spirit-filled seminaries and Spirit-filled Bible study groups. I saw a recent letter to the editors of *Charisma* referring to it as a Spirit-filled magazine.

For these reasons, third-wave Christians do not like to be referred to as Spirit-filled. And for similar reasons, mostly because of the historical baggage it carries, they prefer not to be called charismatic.

3. Experiential distinctives

As we have seen, the doorway to admission into most Pentecostal and charismatic circles is the baptism in the Holy Spirit. Since it is a once-for-all event, it is recalled and celebrated and testified to almost as frequently and precisely as the new birth. This is especially true for those brought up in Christian homes who cannot recall a precise time of conversion.

I was fascinated, for example, as I read Vinson Synan's excellent history of *The Twentieth-Century Pentecostal Explosion*. In it he traces the origin and development of 16 of the contemporary Pentecostal/charismatic movements. It is revealing to notice how the "experience" or the "baptism" furnishes the primary thread that ties them together whether they be Lutheran, Catholic, Foursquare, Methodist or whatever. Just on one page describing the Baptists as a case in point we read, "Clark estimates that at least one third of all the denomination's missionaries [American Baptists] have had a 'charismatic experience.'" And "No one knows how many Southern Baptist pastors and missionaries have received the Pentecostal experience." And "It is also rumored that a high percentage of all Southern Baptist missionaries on the field have spoken in tongues."[11]

The third wave emphasizes no such once-for-all experience that establishes the boundary between belonging or not belonging. The major experiential characteristic for the third wave is ministry, especially healing the sick and casting out demons. And this turns out to be more of a corporate, Body of Christ, emphasis than an individual emphasis, although individual ministry is important. Just how this functions is the major thrust of this book.

THE THIRD WAVE AND EVANGELICALS

The context of the third wave is the evangelical community. Since tens of thousands of words have been written to attempt to define the word *evangelical* to everyone's satisfaction without a great deal of success, I am not particularly inclined to add to the confusion. What I mean by evangelical in this book is uncomplicated. I'm using it in the way most Christian people in the pews are understanding it here and now in America. I simply mean the made-in-Wheaton, *Christianity Today*, Moody Bible Institute, Lausanne Committee, InterVarsity, Gospel Light, Billy Graham, Southern Baptist, Zondervan type of evangelical. It involves a bit of overlapping on the right with fundamentalists and on the left with conciliar evangelicals. I realize that in the broadest sense all Pentecostals and charismatics fit under the evangelical umbrella, but right now I am using the term in a narrower sense, which does not include Pentecostals or charismatics.

If the third wave is to flourish, it must do so primarily among evangelicals as I have described them. But this is not automatic. It does not flow through the evangelical ethos as easily and naturally as a Chuck Swindoll book or a James Dobson film. Decades of anti-Pentecostal rhetoric have raised some formidable barriers. Dave Hunt's *Seduction of Christianity* still tops John Wimber's *Power Evangelism* on current evangelical bestseller lists.

To many evangelicals my explanation of the third wave in this chapter will sound hollow. They will look on it as simply another thinly disguised form of Pentecostalism. After all, doesn't the third wave embrace healings and deliverances from evil spirits? Don't some speak in tongues on a regular basis? Are there not claims to miracles and prophecies and visions and words of knowledge? Isn't the person and work of the Holy Spirit highlighted?

All this sounds suspect to evangelicals who for a couple of generations, in reaction (some of it justified) to excesses in the Pentecostal movement, have been taught what Richard Lovelace of Gordon-Conwell Seminary facetiously calls the doctrine of the modesty of the Holy Spirit. A misunderstanding of John 16:13 has led many to believe that the Holy Spirit never speaks of Himself. Lovelace comments, "Not only were the nine gifts ruled out of the Evangelical movement; it was even dangerous to talk too much about the Holy Spirit."[12]

Evangelical Reformed theology, with roots going back to Benjamin Warfield of Princeton and John Calvin, has taught that the sign gifts such as tongues, interpretation of tongues, healings and miracles ceased with the apostolic age. Although he has since modified his view, John R. W. Stott reflected the general evangelical opinion of the time when he said, at the great World Congress on Evangelism at Berlin in 1966, "The commission of the church is not to heal the sick, but to preach the Gospel.... The church today has no authority to exercise a regular ministry of miraculous healing."[13]

More recently, J. I. Packer, who feels that the jury is still out on whether the sign gifts continued after the apostolic age, says, "The restorationist theory of sign gifts, which the charismatic movement also inherited from older Pentecostalism, is inapplicable; nobody can be sure, nor does it seem likely, that the New Testament gifts of tongues, interpretation, healing and miracles have been restored."[14] I can understand this because it is similar to what I was taught when I studied at Fuller Theological Seminary in the 1950s.

Dispensational theology, which has been featured in many of the nation's outstanding evangelical seminaries and Bible colleges, has reinforced this evangelical mind-set. John F. MacArthur, Jr. says, "Here is a clear biblical word that the miracles, wonders, and sign gifts were given to the first generation apostles to confirm that they were messengers of new revelation."[15]

Dave Breese argues that "The scriptural function of miracles has ceased, in that the written Word of God has already been certified with signs, wonders, miracles, and gifts of the Holy Spirit."[16]

Ray Stedman's view of the signs and wonders and mighty events that we find in the New Testament is that they "were signs that identified the apostles. They were never intended for the church at large."[17]

It is important to understand that none of these evangelical authors, so far as I know, would deny that God does heal today. The question is whether He uses the sign gifts as means to accomplish this ministry. For the large segment of evangelicalism, which has bought in to either the Reformed or the dispensational version of the theory that the sign gifts have ceased, the third wave understandably comes as a threat. However, my perception is that attitudes have been changing over the past 10 years or so.

As contemporary Christian congregations develop their philosophies of ministry, they would do well to let the general public know where they perceive themselves on the spectrum: from charismatic to non-charismatic—open; to non-charismatic—closed; to anti-charismatic. As the years go by, it seems like the trend among evangelicals has been to move away from the anti-charismatic position toward the non-charismatic position. Some of them are open and say, "We welcome practicing charismatics as part of our congregation with the understanding that they are join-ing a non-charismatic church. They may exercise their gifts, but not as part of our official congregational program." Some of them are more closed and say, "We affirm that Pentecostal and charismatic Christianity is a part of God's work in the world today, but we feel it is not for us either in theory or in practice. If you are charismatic you may feel more comfortable in some other church."

I like the way Pastors George Mallone, John Opmeer, Jeff Kirby and Paul Stevens capsulize their pilgrimage. None considers himself as a charismatic pastor of a charismatic church. They admit that "Our backgrounds, both Dispensational and Reformed, taught us to believe that the overt gifts of the Holy Spirit ceased with the apostles. To pass our theological exams we all adopted the party line." Once they left seminary, however, and became involved in ministry for varying periods of time, they found themselves part of the trend I am describing. They have now come to three conclusions:

(1) the cessation of particular gifts was not taught in Scripture; (2) the Church was desperately weak and anemic because of the lack of these gifts; and (3) what we were seeing in our own experience suggested that these gifts were available for the Church today.[18]

This sounds like the third wave to me. Notice, an important factor in changing the minds of these evangelical pastors was their personal experience of God's supernatural power in their ministries. This jibes with my observation that firsthand exposure to a healing, a miracle, a word of knowledge or a deliverance from demons is the most frequent single factor moving evangelicals from skepticism concerning signs and wonders to belief, to openness and then to personal participation in a third-wave type of ministry.

How this very thing happened to me, I will describe in the next chapter.

Notes _____

1. C. Peter Wagner, *On the Crest of the Wave* (Ventura, CA: Regal Books, Div. of Gospel Light Publications, 1983), pp. 19-21.
2. C. Peter Wagner, *Spiritual Power and Church Growth* (Wheaton, IL: Creation House, 1987).
3. Michael Cassidy, *Bursting the Wineskins* (Wheaton, IL: Harold Shaw, 1983), p. 11.
4. James Wong, "Reaching the Unreached," *The Courier*, Mar.-Apr., 1984, p. 6.
5. C. Peter Wagner, "A Third Wave?" *Pastoral Renewal*, July-Aug., 1983, pp. 1-5.
6. Vinson Synan, *In the Latter Days: The Outpouring of the Holy Spirit in the Twentieth Century* (Ann Arbor, MI: Servant Books, 1984), p. 137.
7. David Barrett, World Christian Encyclopedia (New York: Oxford University Press, Inc., 1982).
8. Thomas F. Zimmerman, "Priorities and Beliefs of Pentecostals," *Christianity Today*, Sept. 4, 1981, pp. 36,37.
9. Larry Christenson, "Baptism with the Holy Spirit," *Focus Newsletter*, Fellowship of Charismatic Christians in the United Church of Christ, June 1985, pp. 1-3.
10. Ibid., p. 3.
11. Vinson Synan, *The Twentieth-Century Pentecostal Explosion* (Altamonte Springs, FL: Creation House, 1987), pp. 33-34.
12. Richard Lovelace, "We Need Other Christians," *Charisma*, May 1984, p. 10.
13. John R. W. Stott, "The Great Commission," *One Race, One Gospel, One Task*, Carl F.H. Henry and W. Stanley Mooneyham, eds. (Minneapolis: World Wide Publications, 1967), Vol. 1, p. 51.
14. J. I. Packer, *Keep in Step with the Spirit* (Old Tappan, NJ: Fleming H. Revell Co., 1984), p. 229.
15. John F. MacArthur, Jr., *The Charismatics* (Grand Rapids, MI: Zondervan Academie Books), 1978, p. 78.
16. Dave Breese, *Satan's Ten Most Believable Lies* (Chicago: Moody Press, 1974), p. 86.
17. Ray Stedman, *Acts 1-12: Birth of the Body* (Ventura, CA: Regal Books, Div. of Gospel Light Publications, 1974), p. 105.
18. George Mallone, *Those Controversial Gifts* (Downers Grove, IL: InterVarsity Press, 1983), p. 11.

TWO

HOW I DISCOVERED THE THIRD WAVE

Many people ask me, What is your denominational background?

I have none. I came into Christianity from the pagan pool. I was raised in a happy, well-adjusted family environment where we loved each other very much, but church or God or Jesus or the Bible just wasn't part of our life-style.

It was after I left home for college that I met a young woman named Doris, whom I decided I would like to marry. When I asked her, she told me she couldn't because she had promised God she would only marry a Christian. I responded that I'd be glad to become a Christian. She said there was one more thing: She had also promised God she would be a missionary. Now, I had no clear idea of what a missionary even was, but when she explained, I agreed to that also.

So back in 1950 we knelt together in her parents' farmhouse in upstate New York, where I accepted Jesus as my Savior and Lord and committed myself to missionary service at the same time. She said yes to me, and we are now looking forward to celebrating our thirty-eighth wedding anniversary.

BECOMING EVANGELICALS

While Doris had been brought up in a Christian home, it was a mainline church quite distant from evangelical Christianity. In fact, it was just one week before we met that she had experienced the new birth. So when we were married, we joined the church nearest our home. It was a standard brand denominational church, which will go unnamed at the moment.

We took our church membership seriously; we were elected to lay leadership positions, and we even went to New York City to begin the application process to their foreign mission agency. But then we began to notice that what the minister was preaching was not in accord with what we had been reading in the Bible. He said, for instance, that there was no such thing as hell and that God's love would make sure everyone got to heaven no matter what. As a sermon illustration on another occasion he pulled out a copy of Karl Marx' *Das Kapital*, placed it on the pulpit next to the Bible, and said the two books were equally inspired. While I didn't know much about Christianity then, I knew what he was preaching was not the way I understood it.

At about that time I became aware of InterVarsity

Christian Fellowship; I joined, and was soon introduced to evangelical Christianity. Doris and I transferred our membership to a fundamentalist Bible church where I was later ordained. In order to prepare for our missionary service, we moved to California where I attended Fuller Seminary and Doris attended what is now Biola University. We then served as missionaries in Bolivia under the South America Mission and SIM International (then known as the Andes Evangelical Mission).

With this background, the die had been cast. I had entered into mainstream evangelicalism and have maintained that identity ever since. I have never been inclined to be anything other than an evangelical Christian in the past, nor do I contemplate it in the future.

WHERE WAS THE POWER?

One of the badges of evangelicalism is a high view of the authority of Scripture. What the Bible teaches is regarded as the uncontested rule of faith and practice. I was totally committed to the fulfillment of Jesus' Great Commission: "Go therefore and make disciples of all the nations" (Matt. 28:19). Countless times I had read the words of Jesus that preceded the "therefore" in that passage: "All authority has been given to Me in heaven and on earth" (v. 18). I knew enough Greek to know that the word for authority was *exousia*. I had also read that Jesus had previously given His disciples exousia "over unclean spirits, to cast them out, and to heal all kinds of sickness and all kinds of disease" (10:1). But somehow I had never made any meaningful connection between these passages.

Doris and I spent 16 years in Bolivia as missionaries.

During our first term, out in the jungles near the Brazilian border, I ran a small Bible school, evangelized, planted a church, spoke at Bible conferences and trained Bolivian pastors. We moved to the Andean city of Cochabamba for our second and third terms where I spent most of my time teaching in seminary and in mission administration, directing the mission. By most observers' evaluations we were reasonably competent missionaries, perhaps slightly above average.

But now as we look back on those 16 years, we ask ourselves how many times this power that Jesus talks about for fulfilling the Great Commission, the power that casts out demons and heals the sick, was channeled through us. The answer, so far as we can remember, is not even once.

The question then becomes, why? Where was the power? Since I do not consider myself a spiritual giant, I realize that the answer could well lie in my own lack of consecration to God, the weakness of my prayer habits, my shaky faith or sin in my life. These undoubtedly contributed, but in all honesty I do not believe any of them was the major factor. Strange as it may seem, I believe that the major factor was that I was behaving like most evangelicals were expected to behave in those days. The fact that most of my evangelical friends and colleagues were in the same boat lends credence to my conclusion. As I analyze it, I see at least four major roadblocks keeping me from getting in touch with the power Jesus talked about:

1. *I was a dispensationalist.* I was taught the party line evangelicalism, which I described in the last chapter. I accepted the teaching of leaders such as John Stott, J. I. Packer, John MacArthur, Jr. and Ray Stedman.

I used the Scofield Bible in both English and Spanish where the editor's footnote to 1 Corinthians 13:8 affirmed that the "sign" gifts such as tongues, healings and miracles went out of use after the age of the apostles. I believed that miracles were useful in spreading the gospel before the New Testament was written, but that once the canonical Scriptures were available, they rendered miracles obsolete.

A further aspect of dispensational teaching was that the kingdom of God is seen as future. The church age in which we now live is a sort of parenthesis between the earthly manifestations of the kingdom, which occurred at the time of Jesus' first coming and which will occur again at His second coming. For me, the kingdom was not present here and now, but rather something we hoped for in the future.

2. I was anti-Pentecostal. In my evangelical circles we had agreed that much of what we saw in Pentecostalism was at best a delusion and at worst a fraud. When pressed, we might admit that most Pentecostals would probably end up with us in heaven, but we considered such a judgment an act of Christian generosity, since their theology seemed so shallow to us. I had an aversion, rather than any appreciation, for the Pentecostal-style of ministry. When Pentecostal healers came to Bolivia and set up their tents, I would warn the people in my church not to go to their meetings.

3. I had a limited view of power. When I heard sermons on the power of God, my general assumption was that this power was for salvation, for witnessing and for living a godly life. To go beyond that and include power for healings and miracles was suspect, to say the least, in my circles. It was something that might be expected from those "unenlightened" Pentecostals. It was regarded as somewhat superstitious.

4. I had a humanistic worldview. Since I had received sound, evangelical theological training it would be inaccurate to describe myself as a humanist. But as I look back now, I am amazed at how much the secular humanism of our contemporary American culture has influenced our understanding of Christian theology. A humanistic mind-set has penetrated our Christian schools and seminaries and churches and literature more than we are often ready to admit.

As my colleague, Paul G. Hiebert, points out, we missionaries have often unwittingly served as agents of secularization in the Third World. I can easily identify with that. For example, I can remember feeling that part of my missionary responsibility was to help people in Bolivia see that diseases were caused by germs, not by evil spirits. They could be treated with injections and operations with or without overt reference to God. Sickness and health belonged to the domain of science. Only ignorance would locate them in the domain of the supernatural, and one of the roles of Christianity was to dispel ignorance.

A PARADIGM SHIFT

Now things are decidedly different. On a regular basis I see God's power being used in healing the sick and casting out demons. I am no longer either a dispensationalist nor anti-Pentecostal. I may not have totally shed the influence of secular humanism, but I am aware of the problem and am working on it. I am still an evangelical, but I have now discovered the third wave, and am participating in it.

What brought about the change? It was a process that anthropologist Charles H. Kraft calls a paradigm shift. More of what a paradigm shift entails later on, but suffice it to mention here that my perspective on the operation of the power of God here and now has radically changed. For some, this paradigm shift occurs quite rapidly as a part of a sudden, overpowering filling of the Holy Spirit, or in the aftermath of a dramatic healing. Mine required about 15 years to complete, during which I went through four stages as I began to discover the third wave.

E. Stanley Jones

The first stage was my encounter with the late E. Stanley Jones, the famous Methodist missionary to India. Back in the mid-'60s, Jones had been invited by the local Methodists to come to Bolivia and hold meetings. Not only was I a dispensationalist at that time, I was also a separatistic fundamentalist. I had been taught in seminary that E. Stanley Jones was a liberal, and therefore I wanted no association with him. Our mission, along with several others, had voted in the citywide ministerial association not to welcome him to Cochabamba. The Methodists were left on their own.

But much to my surprise, one of our senior missionaries, a former director of the mission and a widely regarded saint, quietly slipped out to Jones' first meeting. He reported to me the next day that Jones could not be a liberal for he had preached a biblical gospel message, given an invitation and prayed for people to be saved. Since my friend was as fundamentalistic as I was, he aroused my curiosity. The next night Doris and I decided to go and see for ourselves.

I was one of those who had voted in public against E. Stanley Jones, so I planned to be as inconspicuous as possible. I went under cover of darkness, arrived late and slipped in quietly to the back of the room where I could be the first one out. I was shocked. The meeting that night turned out to be an old-fashioned healing service with an invitation to come forward for those who needed healing.

It so happened that I badly needed healing. I had developed a cyst on my neck that had required surgery to remove. Now, I am not the most ideal medical patient, and I almost died when I went into shock shortly after the operation. The surgeon told me it had been an extremely close call. But to make matters worse, the incision would not heal. For weeks it had been a runny, pus-filled sore. And just a couple of days prior to the prayer meeting, the doctor had told me he was going to have to schedule another surgery. That was the last thing I wanted.

So there I was, listening to E. Stanley Jones' invitation for divine healing. His preaching had allowed me to bypass some of my anti-Pentecostal fears and had built my faith in God's power to heal today. But I was the mission director, and I wasn't even supposed to be in the meeting, so I didn't move. Then, after several had gone forward for ministry, Jones did a wonderful thing. He said, "I know there are others who need healing, but for one reason or another you have not come forward. Just relax, because I am going to pray for you also." I took that personally, and as he prayed I had the faith to trust God to heal that incision.

When we got home I took the bandage off. The sore was still open and runny, but I went to bed that night without the bandage. The next morning it was completely healed over, and has been since. The paradigm began to shift—but only slightly.

Pentecostals Are OK

The second stage of my paradigm shift involved church growth research. In the last chapter I mentioned that in the late '60s Donald McGavran had helped me acquire church growth eyes when I studied under him at the Fuller School of World Mission. He instructed his students to study growing churches wherever they may be found, in order to discover principles that in turn might be applied to other churches.

When I returned to Bolivia to apply what I had learned, I found, much to my consternation, that the fastest growing churches in Latin America were the Pentecostals, those I had despised so much. I found that whereas about 20 percent of Latin American evangelicals were Pentecostals in 1950, by 1970 the figure was around 70 percent and rising. This was a phenomenon a church growth leader could not afford to ignore, but I realized that with the reputation I had gained it would not be proper to show any interest in the Pentecostal churches in Bolivia. For example, Bruno Frigoli, the Assemblies of God missionary, had become one of my worst enemies. However, right over on the other side of the Andes Mountains in Chile was a large group of Pentecostals showing explosive growth.

No one knew me in Chile. So with a certain amount of trepidation, I flew over the mountains and attended a few Pentecostal services there. To my amazement these people behaved like true born-again Christians. I observed the fruit of the Spirit in their lives. I talked to their leaders and discovered men and women of God. I asked theological questions and received sensible answers.

The one big difference was their worship services. Unlike the scenario in many of our evangelical churches in Bolivia, those Pentecostals were actually having fun in church! They were singing and dancing in the Spirit, clapping their hands and holding their arms up in the air. Before I knew it, I decided to give it a try, and found myself enjoying it. I heard some tongues and prophecies, and began to think that those gifts might not have gone out with the apostles after all.

The first thing I did when I got back to Bolivia was to make friends with Bruno Frigoli. Soon afterward Doris and I moved back to the United States to begin teaching at Fuller Seminary. That's when I wrote the book now called *Spiritual Power and Church Growth*, sharing what I had learned from Latin American Pentecostals. Writing the book helped me take another large step toward my paradigm shift. And I am pleased to report that book has helped many others do the same.

The Church of God

The third stage of my paradigm shift came about through a period of ministry in the mid-'70s with the Church of God (Cleveland, TN). Their leaders invited me to help them understand and apply church growth principles; this was the first classical Pentecostal denomination I had made contact with over an extended period of time. While they were paying me to teach them, little did they know that I was learning as much as I was teaching. There those men and women of God showed me convincingly that they were in touch with a dimension of the power of God I needed. Every time I visited them I came home spiritually refreshed. At times I even found myself secretly wishing I were a Pentecostal!

Before I finished with the Church of God, I had come to suspect very strongly that God had something different in store for my future.

John Wimber Appears

The fourth and final stage of my paradigm shift came as a result of my contact with John Wimber.

When I first met John in 1975, he was a Quaker pastor who had enrolled in my Doctor of Ministry church growth course. He had already gained a reputation as an effective growth leader in Yorba Linda Friends Church, so I recognized his name when I saw it on the class list. We became acquainted, and after the first week he said, "I've really always known these things you've been teaching, but I never knew what to call them." By the end of the second and final week, I realized that John had possessed an unusually high aptitude as a church growth practitioner and consultant. He was a person I needed.

During the decade of the '70s, I served as the chief executive officer of the Fuller Evangelistic Association as well as an instructor at the seminary. By the middle of the decade I had begun the process of establishing what is now known as the Charles E. Fuller Institute of Evangelism and Church Growth. I did this because, while I was doing fairly well as a church growth theoretician, I realized I needed to team up with a practitioner who knew better than I how to make the theories work on the grass roots level. I saw John Wimber as that person, and I persuaded him to leave his pastorate and come work for me. John got the Charles Fuller Institute off to a fine start, and we became fast friends with a great admiration for each other's gifts and ministries.

At that time both of us were straight-line evangelicals. We had come to the place where we admired Pentecostals and charismatics, but still held them at arm's length. I had a small charismatic-type edge over John in those days since I did use a prayer language from time to time. John had spoken in tongues years before as a new Christian, but had been told that he shouldn't do it anymore, so he didn't. We never discussed it back then, nor did I regard speaking in tongues a central factor in my spiritual life.

Then God called John to plant a new church. I supported the idea, having in mind a small congregation that would help keep him occupied over the weekends when he wasn't out consulting with pastors. Little did I suspect that the new church would eventually grow into Vineyard Christian Fellowship of Anaheim, with over 6,000 members. When God began to bless the church with extraordinary growth, John Wimber was forced to resign his position with the Charles Fuller Institute in 1977. God knew about that, too, and had prepared Carl George of Gainesville, Florida to take John's place and move the Institute ahead from that point. But John and I remained close friends, and every August he continued to help me teach my Fuller Seminary Doctor of Ministry course called Church Growth II.

I became vaguely aware that throughout 1978 to 1980, John and others in his congregation had begun to pray for the sick and see God heal some people. Curious, I visited the church on Sunday nights now and then when it was still meeting in the gymnasium of Canyon High School in Placentia, California. By 1981 John suggested we set aside one of our mornings in Church

Growth II for him to lecture on "Signs, Wonders and Church Growth." If the suggestion had come from almost anyone else, I might have hesitated. This was moving into unchartered territory both in the Church Growth Movement and in Fuller Theological Seminary. But I trusted John Wimber; he had displayed such a high degree of integrity and credibility that I gave him the green light. I made a special point of inviting the dean of our Fuller School of World Mission, Paul E. Pierson, to sit in on the class.

FROM A SPECTATOR TO A PARTICIPANT

Although the lecture was nothing along the lines that Paul Pierson and I had ever heard before, we were both impressed. As we were debriefing over lunch, John mentioned that he had collected much more material on the subject, and we began discussing the possibilities of teaching a whole course on signs and wonders as part of our regular School of World Mission curriculum. Over the next few months the School of World Mission faculty examined the matter at length. Finally a decision was taken to introduce the course: *MC510: Signs, Wonders and Church Growth*. I was to be the professor of record, and John Wimber was to do most of the teaching.

When the class began in January 1982, I carefully assumed the role of spectator. I sat quietly in the last row, watching John "doin' the stuff," as he describes his ministry. I had no intention of doin' the stuff myself.

But all this changed in about the third week. When the teaching was over and the ministry time was beginning, John said, "Is there anyone here who needs prayer for physical healing?" Before I knew it, my hand was in the air. For several years I had been under treatment for high blood pressure and was taking three pills per day. John had me come forward and sit on a stool.

With the class looking on, he began to pray. I felt a tremendous sense of peace come over me. I became so relaxed I feared I might fall off the stool. I dimly heard John giving a sort of play-by-play description of what was happening to me. He was saying, "The Holy Spirit is on him. Can you see the Holy Spirit on him?" I must have been there the better part of 10 minutes. John told me he felt that God was ministering to me, but I should not go off the medication until I had permission from my doctor.

In a few days I went back to my doctor. He was surprised to see my blood pressure so low. I told him what had happened and he listened intently. He said, "That's very interesting. I know unusual things can happen under hypnosis!" He took me off the medication gradually, but in a few months I was taking none.

This finished the process of my paradigm shift. I began as a skeptic, then became a spectator and finally decided to be a participant. I started laying hands on the sick, learning how to minister to them in the name of Jesus. Not many got well at first, but God healed enough of them to encourage me. Soon praying for the sick was a permanent part of my Christian life, even though at that time I did not yet have the gift of healing.

THE 120 FELLOWSHIP

Once I became a participant and began praying for the sick, God showed me that I was to exercise this ministry in a more structured manner. In the summer of 1982, after the first session of MC510 had ended, I helped start a new adult Sunday School class in my church, Lake Avenue Congregational Church in Pasadena, California. None of the original planning for this class included a special ministry of healing the sick. But as it turned out, the class became the major outlet for my personal ministry on the local church level. It also furnished the context in which I have developed most of my ideas on how a third-wave ministry can fit into a traditional evangelical church.

Lake Avenue Congregational Church is one of those traditional evangelical churches. It is 90 years old, and has grown during every one of its nine decades to a church of over 4,000 members, with 3,000 in attendance. Evangelical celebrities such as Wilbur M. Smith, Charles Woodbridge, David Allan Hubbard, Harold Lindsell, Ted Engstrom, Daniel P. Fuller, Ralph D. Winter, Edward Dayton and many others have taught adult Sunday School classes there. It perceives itself clearly as a non-charismatic church.

Without any conscious planning, it just so happened that the week before beginning the new Sunday School class in 1982, I was asked to fill the pulpit for all three morning church services while Pastor Paul Cedar was on vacation. I brought a missionary-type message, sharing with the congregation what God was doing around the world. Part of my reporting included some dramatic stories about supernatural signs and wonders. This sparked the interest of several church members in the new Sunday School class, and 88 were present the first time we met. Through the years the class, called the 120 Fellowship, has been up and down, stabilizing at around 100 on the rolls with an attendance of 80 to 100.

I taught from the book of Acts, and God met us in many unusual—for us—ways. As one class member put it, "We started out studying the book of Acts. Before long, we were living it." Individuals with strong spiritual gifts surfaced over a period of time. God gave us people with gifts of intercession, pastoring, healing, exorcism, prophecy, administration, discernment of spirits, word of knowledge and many others. Several class members developed a habit of sitting under the ministry of John Wimber at Anaheim Vineyard on Sunday nights.

Among the gifted people were George Eckart and Cathy Schaller, whom I put in charge of the class prayer team. Both are disciples of John Wimber. They began a regular time of ministry to the sick after class on Sunday mornings, which has continued through the years.

I believe that God has allowed us to exercise a significant healing ministry in a traditional evangelical church largely for two reasons:

1. The senior pastor, Paul Cedar, is open to the use of all the gifts of the Spirit in the church today. He is supportive of the ministry of the 120 Fellowship, as he is the other 25 adult Sunday School classes, no two of which are just alike. He encourages diversity within the bounds of biblical, evangelical Christianity. He exercises godly wisdom in sensing the moving of the Holy Spirit and in maintaining unity in the Body of Christ.

2. Conscious effort is constantly maintained to avoid the pitfalls of divisiveness listed in the preceding chapter. We do not allow ourselves to be called charismatic or Spirit-filled or anything else that would imply that we are on some sort of spiritual plane superior to other Sunday School classes, which have different types of ministry. We have no "messiah complex," and no hidden agenda to try to alter the philosophy of ministry of the church to conform to our style. Frankly, we like the church the way it is because we feel, as do thousands of others, that it is just about where God wants it to be.

It was within this context that the term *third wave* emerged. If the 120 Fellowship is not charismatic, and if it is different in some ways from the traditional evangelical pattern, then what is it? I like to call it a third-wave group.

THE GIFT OF HEALING

Two years after my paradigm shift had taken place, God gave me the gift of healing. This happened in the summer of 1984 through the ministry of Lutheran pastor Fred Luthy of Lancaster, Pennsylvania.

I met Fred in 1983 when he enrolled in my doctor of ministry course Church Growth I. It was the most unusual session I had ever taught. Fred's own powerful spiritual gift of healing became evident to the whole class almost from the beginning of the two-week session. With my encouragement, Fred conducted an impromptu, informal healing seminar during the breaks and after class. We saw many miraculous works of God during those two weeks.

Fred Luthy returned the following year for Church Growth II. I invited him to dinner in my home with the leaders of the 120 Fellowship prayer team. As the group was about to break up and go home, he asked if anyone there needed prayer for healing. One of the people had a leg somewhat shorter than the other. I was watching with great interest as Fred carefully measured the legs and prepared to ask God to even them. But he suddenly turned to me and said, "I think God wants you to pray for this leg." So I did and it instantly lengthened. God used me to heal two other cases of short legs and back pains that day.

As I explain in *Your Spiritual Gifts Can Help Your Church Grow*, I do not believe that seeing God move in a way like this is necessarily evidence that one has a particular spiritual gift. It may be something God chooses to do once or twice, and that's it. I was open to the possibility that it might be a gift, but I needed more experimentation to find out for sure. So after prayer and consultation with others I asked God to give me some clear evidence over the next four months (the remainder of 1984) as to whether He had given me the gift of healing or not.

Many things happened over those four months pointing toward a positive answer. Two were so unusual that they continue to stand out in my mind.

The first took place in one of John Wimber's Vineyard Christian Fellowship training conferences. I was invited to address a banquet meeting in a hotel with about 1000 pastors and spouses present. During the worship session I felt an overpowering presence of the Holy Spirit and God spoke to me directly in my spirit telling me to conduct a mass healing. I had never even thought about such a thing previously, but I knew I must obey God. As a result, at least 50 people who had short legs, back pains and other skeletal problems were healed that night.

The second unusual event happened when Paul Yonggi Cho came to Pasadena to deliver the annual Church Growth Lectures at the Fuller School of World Mission. Cho, a longtime friend, is pastor of the world's largest church, the Yoido Full Gospel Church of Seoul,

Korea, which has a membership of over 500,000. In private conversation he mentioned that he had heard God was using me to lengthen legs, and that he would like to see me do it. Sure enough, the next day God sent in an Egyptian Coptic pastor who as a teenager had been run over by a train, and whose leg had been stiff, weak, deformed and short ever since. God moved powerfully, and in Cho's presence the pastor's leg lengthened, and he was able to place his full weight on it for the first time since the accident.

> *I believe all Christians have the role of laying hands on the sick and being open to see God use them as channels for healing.*

Cho later told the story to his congregation in Seoul. A deaconess whose hip sockets had been disintegrating listened intently. During the sermon she believed she heard God tell her to go to Pasadena to have Peter Wagner pray for her. She checked with Pastor Cho and he agreed; so she came. She entered my seminary office on a crutch, and left walking without it. A week later, just before returning to Korea, she showed me X-rays that had been taken before and after the prayer, and pointed to places where the doctor had indicated there was new bone tissue growing in the hip sockets.

God has given me the gift of healing, and I use it whenever I can. Not that everyone I pray for is improved, but as I will document later on in the book, many do get better. By the way, I do not believe that the gift of healing is a prerequisite to pray for the sick, but rather all Christians have the role of laying hands on the sick and being open to see God use them as channels for healing.

However, those to whom God chooses to give the gift experience on the one hand an added dimension of power for healing, but on the other hand they assume added responsibility and accountability. It is all a matter of stewardship. To whom much is given much is required (see Luke 12:48).[1]

WILL THE THIRD WAVE FLOURISH?

I am sure it will not take everyone 15 years to discover the third wave. Although some might even need more than 15 years, I suspect that most will do it much more rapidly. However long the process takes, there are six stages that can be clearly discerned:

1. Opposition. Relatively few Christians find themselves at the extreme position of actively opposing ministries of the miraculous, although some do.

2. Unbelief. To many Christians, particularly among those who interpret their faith with humanistic presuppositions, the idea of God intervening directly in human affairs is absurd. They do not particularly oppose those who believe in the miraculous, they simply feel sorry for them.

3. Skepticism. The skeptic admits the possibility of the miraculous, but doubts whether God has very often, if ever, acted through signs and wonders. In theory they affirm miracles; in practice, probably not.

4. Belief. Most evangelical Christians believe that Mary conceived without sexual intercourse, that God saved Daniel from the lions and that Jesus walked on water. Some go beyond this, however, and believe that we may expect God to work in similar ways in our churches today.

5. *Openness to others.* At this stage we affirm that, yes, legitimate healings and other miracles are taking place in many churches and in the ministry of many individuals today. We are supportive, even at times enthusiastic, about what God is doing through signs and wonders, but we prefer to be spectators rather than participants.

6. *Participation in ministry.* We actively engage in a ministry of miraculous healing, sometimes as individuals and sometimes as part of a group of like-minded Christians.

I believe that more and more Christians these days are moving toward Stage 6. My particular ministry, including this book, begins at Stage 4—belief, and aims toward Stage 6—participation. Others, however, such as my Fuller Seminary colleague Colin Brown, go much deeper and attempt to help people move from Stages 1, 2 or 3 to belief in a God who is a God of miracles. Brown's book *Miracles and the Critical Mind,* is a persuasive scholarly examination of the standard objections to miracles. Then he popularizes his arguments in language that all can understand in the smaller book *That You May Believe.*

A while ago I was quoted in *USA Today* as saying that I felt by the end of the century praying for the sick in our churches would be about as common as Sunday School. Many friends have asked me if I really believe that, and I do. The current trend among Christians is clearly toward Stage 6. Not everyone at Stage 6 will identify with the third wave, but a significant number will, in my judgment. That is why I think the third wave will, in fact, flourish in our times.

POSITIVE SIGNS

As we move toward the twenty-first century, some fairly clear features of the Christian landscape point in the direction of more openness to the New Testament work of the Holy Spirit both in theory and in practice. As I see them, there are at least five major features that lead to these conclusions:

1. More liberals are becoming evangelicals. Liberal Christianity peaked two or three decades ago. New adult conversions to Christianity worldwide are almost all in churches that consider themselves theologically conservative. On many occasions as I have ministered in pastors' conferences and talked personally with pastors, one or another has remarked rather casually, "When I was still a liberal . . . . " The Pentecostal and charismatic movements have stimulated this trend considerably.

Even some of those who remain liberal are nevertheless opening up to the phenomena of supernatural signs and wonders and healing ministries. In a recent issue of the *International Review of Mission,* for example, World Council of Churches executive Arne Sovik reviews six books on healing written by conciliar-type authors. In his opening comments he says, "It is only relatively recently that there has been a revival of serious interest in the study of what part one's faith has in healing." Then he makes this very revealing statement: "Until a decade or two ago it would seem that the major function of the hospital chaplain was not to be a part of the healing team but rather to prepare the patient for the eventuality that healing might not come."[2] Obviously, things are different now.

Pastor Vic Varkoni of East Presbyterian Church in

Charlotte, North Carolina is participating in the same trend. He says, "The most distinctive aspect of my congregation's ministry is healing." He thanks God for bringing healing even though they did not ask for it or plan for it. He considers it unusual because, "We are not evangelical or charismatic, but we are being healed . . . . We Presbyterians just don't expect this."[3]

Because of their commitment to biblical authority, evangelicals are not debating one another as to the validity of the miraculous. The question, however, is whether we are to expect the miraculous in our ministry today.

2. Evangelicals believe in miracles. Because of their commitment to biblical authority, evangelicals are not debating one another as to the validity of the miraculous. The question, however, is whether we are to expect the miraculous in our ministry today. More and more are finding that the step from believing in miracles in general to believing in miracles today is not that great.

3. Evangelicals believe in demons. Even among evangelicals who argue that the charismatic movement is unbiblical and who teach that gifts of tongues and prophecies and healings and miracles were discontinued after the apostolic age, a large number realistically admit that demons are active today and need to be dealt with. Moody Bible Institute, for example, has been at the center of American dispensationalism and has been publicly anti-charismatic. Nevertheless Moody Press has published two of the finest books available on deliverance from demons: Mark I. Bubeck's *The Adversary* and

Overcoming the Adversary. I use both in my classes at Fuller Seminary. More recently the chairperson of Moody's Theology Department, C. Fred Dickason, has published *Demon Possession and the Christian* relating, among other things, how he has personally ministered to over 400 demonized Christian brothers and sisters.

4. *Evangelicals believe that God heals today.* Theologically speaking, there should not be a great deal of distance between believing that God casts out demons supernaturally today and believing that He heals disease supernaturally today. And this is the case. When it comes right down to it, few, if any, evangelicals would assert that God cannot or does not heal today. Most all, if so requested, would follow the guidelines laid down in James 5:13-15 about calling the elders and anointing with oil and praying the prayer of faith. But, realistically speaking, expectations for miraculous healing among evangelicals are not typically very high. Elmer L. Towns graphically describes it when he says, "Neither minister nor patient expects a dramatic intervention by God. The pastor prays weakly, 'Lord, bless the doctors and give them wisdom. Lay your healing hand on your child. Amen.'" Towns goes on to comment, "There does not seem to be much faith or healing."[4]

The October 1982 issue of *Christian Life* magazine featured the MC510 course at Fuller Seminary, "Signs, Wonders and Church Growth." As a result the publishers experienced the greatest reaction to a single feature in the magazine's history. Because of popular demand it was reprinted several times.[5] The publishers followed it up with a survey of the opinions of major evangelical leaders nationwide. One of the questions was: Do you believe "signs and wonders" as alluded to in the New

Testament are for today? Of 29 distinguished leaders representing the spectrum of evangelicalism, only two answered in the negative. By no means would all of the 27 positive responses identify with the first, second or third waves, but at the same time they are not awfully far away.

5. *Evangelicals are listening to Pentecostals and charismatics.* For quite some time, evangelicals in general treated the Pentecostal and charismatic movements with benign indifference, not to mention hostility. But the massive growth of those movements, which I will describe in the next chapter, has now made this all but impossible. I like the way veteran evangelical missiologist J. Herbert Kane of Trinity Evangelical Divinity School puts it. "Until recently, many evangelicals rejected signs and wonders; they did so on theological grounds . . . . But all this is beginning to change." He points out that evangelicals were attempting to use apostolic methods on the mission field, but, "Alas, we forgot that apostolic methods, without apostolic power, are no better than any other methods." What is bringing about the change in thinking? Kane says, "Our charismatic and Pentecostal friends have helped us immensely in this area and we owe them a debt of gratitude."[6]

THIRD-WAVE TEACHING IN SEMINARIES

One of the most positive signs of the acceptance of third-wave teaching among evangelicals is the willingness of seminaries and Bible schools to experiment with related courses. The MC510 course John Wimber and I pioneered at Fuller Seminary has already been mentioned. During the four years the course was taught, a negative reaction had built up among some theology professors, and the course had to be canceled for a year. A special commission of 12 professors studied the matter for eight months and produced an 80-page joint statement. Then in 1987 a similar course was reinstated—*MC550: The Ministry of Healing and World Evangelization*, taught jointly by Charles H. Kraft and myself. It has been and continues to be one of the most popular elective courses in the seminary.

Timothy M. Warner of Trinity Evangelical Divinity School in Deerfield, Illinois introduced, in the fall of 1985, *ME875M: Power Encounter in Missionary Ministry*. It explores biblical concepts of power as they relate to God, Christ, the Holy Spirit, angels, Satan and demons. The hows and whys of spiritual warfare are taught. This course was expected to attract about 25 students, considered a good enrollment for an elective course at Trinity. Instead 81 students showed up, making it one of the school's largest elective courses. Also at Trinity, Kenneth S. Kantzer has begun teaching a course on the history of the charismatic movement.

At Columbia Biblical Seminary and Graduate School of Missions in Columbia, South Carolina Philip M. Steyne teaches *MIS624: A Biblical Theology of Power Encounter*. He deals with the nature of the encounter between divine and satanic powers especially as it occurs in human experience.

F. Douglas Pennoyer of Seattle Pacific University is developing a course on "The Devil, Demons, and World Missions." *PT802 Spiritual Warfare* is taught in the Practical Theology Department of Biola's Talbot School of Theology by Professor Neil Anderson, and the Biola undergraduate program offers *Anthropology 401 Magic, Witchcraft and Sorcery*. Moody Bible Institute offers *SK3502 Counselling: Spirit Oppression* taught by C. Fred Dickason and Mark I. Bubeck. Other institutions are adding their names to the list.

By mentioning this, I do not mean to imply that all of the above institutions would endorse the conclusions of this book. Some would regard me as overly charismatic. But, still, the intensity of disagreement is not nearly as sharp and defensive as it was even 10 years ago.

Much of this new trend is emerging from the missions faculties of these schools. Theological faculties have been a bit more reticent to agree that such teaching is useful. That is why a word from John Jefferson Davis, professor of systematic theology at Gordon-Conwell Theological Seminary in South Hamilton, Massachusetts, is so timely. Davis, in surveying future directions for American evangelicals, admits, "Those of us who, like myself, stand within the Reformed theological tradition have much to learn from the Wesleyan, Holiness and Pentecostal experiences of the Spirit." He discusses and defines the term *power evangelism*, and says, "Worldwide there has been a growing trend since about 1950 toward the recognition and practice of power evangelism."[7]

Does this seminary teaching make a difference?

It does in the ministry of George and Gayle Weinand who work as missionaries in San Jose, Costa Rica. After taking the MC510 course at Fuller, they wrote home saying, "Since our return to Costa Rica in January, we have been operating in a new power we never knew in our previous six years here." They tell how they ministered to an epileptic woman who had been involved in witchcraft, the Quija board and the occult. They cast the demons out of her, and "now after 46 years of torment, she is totally free."

The Weinands go on to tell of a man with a hernia so bad he could hardly walk; he was instantly healed when they prayed for him. Another was healed of a broken wrist. A Bible school student suffering demonic attacks of homosexuality was delivered and his life has been changed.

They conclude the letter by saying, "This is that magnetic power of the early church, that the Lord is stirring up in many parts of the world. It's happening now in Costa Rica, and we are greatly encouraged."[8]

So am I.

Notes _____

1. Some of the material in the preceding section has previously appeared in my chapter "Discovering the Power" in *Power Encounters Among Christians in the Western World* edited by John Wimber and Kevin Springer (Harper & Row) due Spring 1988.
2. Arne Sovik, "Signs and Wonders," *International Review of Mission*, April 1987, p. 271.
3. Vic Varkoni, "We Are Being Healed," *Monday Morning*, May 19, 1986, p. 15.
4. Elmer L. Towns, "Does God Heal Today?" *Fundamentalist Journal*, June 1983, p. 36.
5. An updated and expanded version of the October 1982 issue of *Christian Life* is now available in book form: *Signs and Wonders Today*, edited by C. Peter Wagner (Altamonte Springs, FL: Creation House, 1987).
6. J. Herbert Kane, *Wanted: World Christians* (Grand Rapids, MI: Baker Book House, 1986), pp. 214-216.
7. John Jefferson Davis, "Future Directions for American Evangelicals," *Journal of the Evangelical Theological Society*, Dec. 1986, p. 464.
8. George and Gayle Weinand, San Jose, Costa Rica, May 1985 prayer letter.

THREE

POWER EVANGELISM TODAY

Most Christians sincerely seek the answer to the question: Just what is it that God is doing in the world today? And rightly so.

This issue is extraordinarily important because, as the Bible teaches, the wind of the Holy Spirit blows where it wishes (see John 3:8). What God was doing in the world yesterday is not necessarily what He is doing today. That is why Jesus says, "He who has an ear, let him hear what the Spirit says to the churches" (Rev. 2:7).

SEEING IS BELIEVING

In the last chapter I mentioned that one of the keys to my personal paradigm shift from anti-Pentecostal to a participant in the third wave was an honest appraisal of the Pentecostal movement in Latin America. The phenomenal growth of those churches, far surpassing the growth of the type of churches I was associated with, attracted my attention. A close examination subsequently convinced me that I was observing an extraordinary work of the Holy Spirit. The question to me became: Do I have an ear to hear what the Spirit is saying to the churches?

I was not alone. Donald A. McGavran, regarded by many as the twentieth-century's outstanding missiologist, has dedicated his life to observing and analyzing the growth and nongrowth of churches around the world. Through most of his active career, which spanned the 55 years between 1925 and 1980, his reaction to stories of miraculous healings was that of "any ordinary normal American." He believed that if you're sick, you go to a hospital. "The suggestion that you call somebody and have him anoint you with oil and pray over you," he says, "is often regarded as superstitious." He, of course, would not deny that such teaching was in the Bible. And, he would admit, "Maybe in another dispensation, a long time ago, it worked. But not today."

His attitude changed in the 1960s, however, around the time he became the founding dean of the Fuller Seminary School of World Mission in Pasadena, California. His ongoing research was showing that the most rapidly growing churches were those that opened themselves wide to the action of the Holy Spirit. He now says, "The evidence I uncovered in country after country—

including North America—simply would not permit me to hold my former point of view. And I may say that, as I meditated on it, my biblical convictions wouldn't permit it."[1]

It is hard for some to recognize how radical a change such thinking is from the past. For example, Rufus Anderson, one of the famous missiologists of the last century, expresses the wisdom of his times when he writes, in 1869, that missionaries cannot be regarded as contemporary apostles because they "lack the 'signs and wonders and mighty deeds,' which St. Paul, in his Second Epistle to the Corinthians, declares to be the needful 'signs of an apostle.'"[2]

Never in history has such a high percentage of the world's population been exposed to the gospel, nor the increase of evangelical Christians been so encouraging.

McGavran tells of a revealing conversation with Methodist Bishop Waskom Pickett of India back in the 1930s. Pickett said that as he researched his book *Christian Mass Movements* in India (1936), he "found more miracles, signs and wonders than in the book of Acts."

McGavran asked, "Why didn't you tell about them in your book?"

"If I had," Pickett replied, "no one would have believed the rest of the book."

He was probably right. The Pentecostal movement had just begun, and many Christians of the day sincerely doubted that it was a legitimate work of the Holy Spirit. But no longer.

THE POWER BEHIND THE HARVEST

As I mentioned in chapter 1, the closing years of the twentieth century are witnessing the greatest growth of worldwide Christianity that has ever been known. Researcher Patrick Johnstone says, "The harvest of people into the Kingdom of God in recent years has been unprecedented. Never in history has such a high percentage of the world's population been exposed to the gospel, nor the increase of evangelical Christians been so encouraging."[3]

The influential evangelical periodical *Christianity Today* recently took note of this phenomenon and assigned Sharon E. Mumper to do a cover story. The introductory section of her article, "Where in the World Is the Church Growing?" opens with the story of a miraculous healing in China, pointing out that such an occurrence is far from unusual today. Mumper says, "Healings, exorcisms, and other supernatural signs and wonders have accompanied phenomenal growth of the church not only in China, but in many other surprising parts of the world."[4]

All this fits in with my own findings after a sizable two-year research project assigned by the Zondervan Publishing House as part of their *Dictionary of the Pentecostal and Charismatic Movements*.[5] When I began, I knew that Pentecostals and charismatics were growing rapidly, but I was not fully prepared for what I found. While figures continually change because of new discoveries of pockets of growth by researchers, we do have a fairly dependable fix up to 1985. During the first 40 years or so of the movement, Pentecostals and charismatics had grown to around 16 million in 1945, good growth but not spectacular. Then an acceleration began, and in the second 40 years they increased to some 247 million. Over the last 10 years of the period (1975 to 1985), they increased from 96 million to 247 million, a decadal growth rate (DGR) of 157 percent. What does this mean in perspective? Admitting that I am not a professional historian, I will nevertheless risk the following hypothesis: *No other nonpolitical, non-militaristic human movement in history has grown as rapidly as the Pentecostal/charismatic movement has over the past 40 years.* Even if some historian falsifies my hypothesis, my point in making it will remain, namely, that if this is a contemporary work of the Holy Spirit, which I am fully convinced it is, Christian leaders are making a grievous error if they fail to lend an ear to what the Spirit is saying to the churches.

I am not suggesting that we all join the Pentecostal or charismatic movements. But I am suggesting that we join the movement of the Holy Spirit. The third wave is a more feasible option for many. As we have seen, researcher David Barrett estimates 27 million third-wavers need to be added to the above figures to get a fuller picture of what God is doing in the world.

Not that this is all God is doing, I hasten to add. As I have mentioned previously, there are places in the world where vigorous church growth is taking place without signs and wonders. Take, for example, the churches in Guatemala associated with the Central American Mission (CAM). The founder of CAM was none other than C. I. Scofield, the editor of the study Bible that carries his name and that teaches that the sign gifts went out of use with the close of the apostolic age. The mission, closely linked with Dallas Theological Seminary, has maintained an anti-Pentecostal stance throughout the years. Still, their churches have grown well under the blessing of God. Their baptized members increased from 38,480 in 1980 to 49,584 in 1983, a DGR of 138 percent.[6]

Many other examples could be given, such as Singapore where the second most rapidly growing group of churches, after the Pentecostals, is the Bible Presbyterian Church, a staunchly anti-Pentecostal denomination.

WHERE GOD IS MOVING

Worldwide, every story of non-Pentecostal church growth can be matched by perhaps a dozen stories of Pentecostal and charismatic church growth. The growth of one denomination, the Assemblies of God, over the past 20 years provides a case history of expansion unparalleled in modern times. In 1965 they counted 16,000 churches as compared to 107,415 in 1985. Membership grew from around 1.5 million to over 13 million over the same 20 years, and these represent almost excessively conservative figures. This translates to a DGR of 194 percent. The denomination is growing so rapidly that already it constitutes the largest or second largest Protestant denomination in no less than 30 nations of the world. In Sao Paulo, Brazil alone, the Assemblies of God report 2,400 congregations, more than some entire U.S. national denominations, such as Christian and Missionary Alliance or Baptist General Conference.

When Paul Yonggi Cho's Yoido Full Gospel Church in Seoul, Korea added the 100,000th member in 1979, it was like breaking the four-minute mile. Cho had shown the world that metachurches—churches of several tens of thousands—were possible. Especially during the decade of the '80s, many other megachurches—churches of several thousands—and meta-churches have appeared. While not all of them are Pentecostal or charismatic, a reasonable guess would be that probably 80 percent of them are.

Miracles in Metachurches

One of the fastest growing metachurches is the Sung Rak Baptist Church of Seoul, Korea, pastored by Ki Dong Kim. Since it traces its ancestry to the U.S. Southern Baptists, it is not included in the usual Pentecostal or charismatic statistics. David Barrett counts it in his category of third wave. In 1987 it passed the 40,000-member mark; a sanctuary seating 20,000 is planned. Pastor Kim testifies to being used to raise 10 people from the dead, casting out thousands of demons and seeing 59 totally crippled people who are now walking.

Recently, I had the privilege of preaching for Pastor Kim in one of the six Sunday worship services. Some 4,000 attended that service leaving not a single empty seat. Toward the end 150 men and women came forward to commit their lives to Jesus Christ, and they were led out to an instructional class by Deacon Shin Cho Kim. Deacon Kim was a North Korean commando who, along with 30 others, invaded South Korea in 1968 with the assignment of assassinating President Park. The South Korean guards apprehended them, and as a result of the ensuing battle, 30 of the North Koreans were killed. Only Shin Cho Kim survived, and he was imprisoned for five years.

After serving his sentence, Kim married a South Korean woman who was a backslidden Baptist. But she fell ill with cancer of the stomach and was told that she would die. Desperate, she got up courage enough to ask

Pastor Ki Dong Kim to pray for her, and, as a result, she was completely healed. She quickly decided to repent of her sins and return to Christ and to the church. Her husband was an atheist, however, and wanted nothing to do with Christianity. But she was able to persuade him to go with her to church to celebrate her birthday, and he was impressed. He soon got to meet Pastor Kim, who prayed for him and cast out three demons. Shin Cho Kim immediately opened his heart to Jesus and was saved. God then gifted him as a powerful lay evangelist, and since then he has seen over 15,000 persons come to Christ under his ministry. He also serves as the president of the South Korean anti-Communist league!

Dramatic stories of power evangelism such as these are emerging from virtually every area of the globe. One of the largest local churches in Africa is the Deeper Life Bible Church of Lagos, Nigeria, pastored by W. F. Kumuyi. Located in the center of the city, it meets in a gigantic sanctuary seating over 13,000 and is filled several times each Sunday. In 1986 the church reported 42,000 members, up from 1,500 members 10 years previously. One of the reasons for its explosive growth is that word of the healing power of God has spread throughout the city. Deeper Life member John Danuma, for example, had suffered from leprosy for years. As he tells it, "literally every part of my body had been eaten off. My thighs were the worst. They were mutilated. My flesh was like frog's skin. Nauseating odors exuded from my body . . . . Eating was as painful as death."[7]

And then Ma Celina's body had also been wracked with leprosy for 25 years. "The stench became more rancid. Fingers were dropping off. The pains were more gruesome than the pangs of death," she testifies.[8] In his day, as we know, Jesus encountered many such people who had given up all hope. In Nigeria, the medical doctors, the native doctors and the acupuncturists could do nothing. Friends took John Danuma and Ma Celina to the Deeper Life Bible Church almost against their will. In each case Pastor Kumuyi prayed, and each felt a cold sensation throughout their body. Both were dramatically healed and, as a result, became faithful Christians.

In Europe and Africa the most vigorously growing churches are most commonly of the Pentecostal/charismatic variety. The so-called house church movement, the independent charismatics of England, is leading the way in growth in that nation. Between 1980 and 1985 the number of churches increased from 190 to 650, accommodating some 75,000 members. The largest and fastest growing church in Sweden is the Charismatic Word of Life Community in Uppsala. Pastor Ulf Ekman has constructed a sanctuary of 4,000, said to be the largest Protestant church building in Europe. In Norway 20 percent of the practicing Christians are now charismatic, with the percentage even higher among those who are college educated. In Italy, over 80 percent of the Protestants are affiliated with the Assemblies of God.

In Latin America evangelicals in general are growing from a mere 50,000 at the beginning of our century to a projected 137 million by the end of the century. This remarkable church growth, much more rapid than the growth of the population in general, is increasingly spearheaded by Pentecostal churches. While Pentecostals constituted about 25 percent of evangelicals at mid-century, the figure toward the end of the century has risen to around 80 percent. In 13 of the 20 major Latin American republics, a Pentecostal denomination was the largest of the Protestant groups reported in 1985, and they were close seconds in four others. The world's second largest church is the Evangelical Cathedral of Jotabeche in Santiago, Chile, pastored by Javier Vasquez. Their 1986 report lists over 300,000 baptized members. They meet in their main sanctuary, which seats 16,000, as well as in a network of 384 branch churches scattered throughout a 10-mile radius.[9] Healing is a major factor in the growth of the Jotabeche church, and some of that healing ministry is unusual for a Pentecostal church. Since this is a Methodist Pentecostal church, many traditions of Methodism remain, including infant baptism. Because of their Roman Catholic culture, most Chilean parents wish to have their infants baptized, but many cannot afford the fees charged by the Catholic Church. Not only are the Jotabeche pastors willing to do it free, but numerous sick children are healed through prayers offered at the baptism. Numbers of children declared terminally ill by medical doctors and some legally dead have been raised up to new life, and the word gets around.

Outside of Korea, the growth of Asian megachurches is fairly recent. But within the past 10 years such churches as Calvary Church of Kuala Lumpur, Malaysia, pastored by Prince Guneratnam and Calvary Charismatic Center of Singapore, pastored by Rick Seaward, and the Hope of Bangkok Church in Thailand, pastored by Kriengsak Chareonwongsak, represent many new, burgeoning Pentecostal or charismatic churches throughout the region. The Hope of Bangkok Church, with over 2,000 active members, is many times the size of any other church in the country, and Pastor Kriengsak's aggressive vision is to plant at least one new church in each of Thailand's 685 provinces by the year 2000.

The Amazing Jesus *Film*

Speaking of Thailand, the most vigorous multiplication of churches in the nation's history began in 1982 when Campus Crusade for Christ introduced their *Jesus* film. If their reports are accurate, more churches have been started in Thailand in the decade of the 1980s than in the 160 years of previous missionary effort. But the effect of the *Jesus* film is being felt in many parts of the world besides Thailand. It is reported that currently at least 150,000 persons view the film every day, resulting in at least 15,000 decisions for Christ. While not all of these become ongoing disciples of Christ, an increasingly significant number are being folded into home Bible fellowship groups and new churches. If I were asked to nominate my candidate for the most effective evangelistic tool in the world today, I would have to nominate this film.

Why is the *Jesus* film so powerful? For one thing, the highest quality of acting, photography and film production has been utilized. Second, the script for the film comes entirely from the Gospel of Luke. It is the Word of God unencumbered by Hollywood frills, and, as we know, faith comes by hearing and hearing by the Word of God (see Rom. 10:17). Third, no expense has been spared in providing state-of-the-art computerized lip synchronization into the vernacular of the people.

So what does this all mean? It means very little, as a matter of fact, in technological societies such as the U.S. Few American pastors even know of the film, and those who have seen it have not been overly impressed. But the situation is totally different in non-technological areas of the Third World. When the film is shown, sometimes against the whitewashed wall of a building, in a remote village of India or Nepal the effect is dramatic. As far as many of those people are concerned, Jesus and His disciples have visited their village in person. When they see Jesus healing the sick and casting out demons, they are deeply impressed, because what He does relates so directly to their daily life. Many people they know and love are sick and demonized, including themselves in many cases. No one is around to raise problems of textual criticism or to mention Bultmann's theories of demythologization or to warn that what Jesus did was for a past dispensation, as we are accustomed to hearing in many of our Western churches today. No. For them at the top of their agenda is fear of evil spirits, and a chief felt need is for power to overcome their influence. Apparently this Jesus who has come to visit them has such power.

This is power evangelism at its best, because it is so similar to the way Jesus did it. While most will agree that the gospel has dimensions of both word and deed, for many of us rationally oriented Westerners, the word comes first and is followed by the deed. But this is not the normal sequence for many of the peoples described in the New Testament, nor for many in the world today. Even secular historians are beginning to recognize where early Christianity got its power for church growth. For example, Yale University Historian Ramsay MacMullen raises the question: What did Christianity present to its audience? As he analyzes the Christianization of the Roman Empire, he finds that the deed in the early centuries of the expansion of Christianity far exceeded the word in evangelistic effectiveness. He affirms that divine power especially in casting out demons "had a terrifying high-voltage quality," and should be seen as the chief instrument of conversion in those first centuries.[10]

"Jesus, Show Me Your Power"

MacMullen could have been describing the *Jesus* film in India. As Campus Crusade executive Paul Eshleman relates in his book on the *Jesus* film, *I Just Saw Jesus*, a Hindu witch doctor (*bhaghat*) in Mandala, India saw the film and was fascinated by the power that Jesus and even His disciples had in the realm of the supernatural. When he went home, he tore the picture of Jesus off the flyer advertising the film and placed it on his god shelf next to his favorite gods. The more he thought of it, the more he wondered if Jesus could really be the one true God as He claimed. So he decided on a test. He placed a ball of cow dung fuel in front of each god on the shelf and stepped back, saying in so many words, "All right, Jesus, if you're the one true God, show me your power." Almost immediately the ball of cow dung in front of the picture of Jesus burst into flame. Needless to say, the rest of the gods were promptly discarded, and the man became a faithful follower of Jesus.[11]

Stories like this have been multiplied in reports by Campus Crusade personnel around the world. In the Solomon Islands, for example, a couple whose little girl was given up to die by the doctors saw Jesus raise Jairus's daughter from the dead. They went home and prayed for their daughter, and she was completely healed.[12]

In Thailand a gang of murderous bandits attacking a group of Christians was halted in their tracks by the physical appearance of two angels with flaming swords. In another part of Thailand the film team had to sleep in a Buddhist temple known by all to be inhabited by demons. That night, one of the demons appeared to them, they cast it out in the name of Jesus, and slept peacefully, much to the astonishment of the villagers.[13] In India, Nazarene Pastor S. Dinakaran reports that some evil spirits kept blowing out the projector bulbs and tearing the screen until they were dealt with directly and forced to stop by the direct power of God.[14]

Little wonder the gospel is now spreading rapidly in places previously considered highly resistant. Nepal, for instance, is a nation closed to the gospel. Converting Nepalese to Christ is against the law. But when people see the *Jesus* film and take Jesus' words and works literally as recorded in the Gospel of Luke, amazing things happen. Not only do they commit their lives to Jesus, but they are unsophisticated enough to believe that Jesus will heal the sick and cast out demons through them. And they are delighted to discover that He does. Power evangelism is now so effective in Nepal that the number of baptized believers has grown from a mere 500 in 1976 to over 60,000 in 1986—just 10 years later, and the rate continues to increase. Some whole villages have become Christian.

Interestingly enough, most of these believers, affiliated with the Nepal Christian Fellowship, do not identify themselves as Pentecostal or charismatic. They probably fit more easily into the third wave.

Power Evangelism in China

The two hottest spots of the expansion of the kingdom of God in the world today are China and Argentina. The growth of Christianity in China, which began to accelerate greatly in 1976, has broken all the records. When the Communists took over and drove out the missionaries in 1949 and 1950, an estimated 1 million Protestant believers were left behind. Then some of the most severe persecution since the days of Nero set in. Pastors were arrested and jailed, Bibles were burned, churches and homes used for meetings were closed down, Christians were harassed and discriminated against and beaten. The work of Chairman Mao and the Red Guard and the Gang of Four should have been enough to wipe Christianity out of China for good. But it wasn't. The Holy Spirit remained, the house church movement began to flourish, and, as I mentioned in the first chapter, a conservative estimate of the current number of believers in China is now 50 million. The Christian community comprises between 5 and 10 percent of the population, and is growing rapidly. Reports state that between 10,000 and 20,000 persons are becoming Christians every day.

How is this happening? Many excellent books have been coming off the presses analyzing this extraordinary phenomenon.[15] There are several factors that have contributed strongly, such as the faithful witness of believers through suffering, itinerant preaching especially by women, the purity of the church maintained through strict discipline, Christian radio broadcasting, the failure of either Confucianism or Marxism to meet basic human needs and others. But all the authors agree that none of these factors has been more important than the supernatural power released through signs and wonders. Strong ministry in healing and casting out demons had not previously been such a significant part of the traditional Protestant churches in China, although examples of it could be found here and there. But things changed once the Western missionaries left. With no special planning or preaching or exhortation in that direction, powerful manifestations of supernatural signs and wonders spontaneously burst forth in every single province of China. Ministries of the miraculous became a normal part of Christian experience, much as they were in the book of Acts. They are now almost taken for granted.

Jonathan Chao, founding director of the Chinese Church Research Center in Hong Kong, lectured on signs and wonders in the Chinese Church at Fuller Seminary in 1986. Among many documented reports was one that occurred in the latter years of the counter-revolution (1973 to 1976). At that time it was a crime against the state to believe in Jesus. A Christian mother had taken her baby to the hospital where it had died. Instead of burying the corpse, the mother took it home, held it in her arms and prayed over it for four days and nights. At the end of the fourth day, God answered her prayers and raised the baby from the dead. The doctor and the nurse who had signed the death certificate had no mental categories to relate to what had actually happened before their eyes. Many believed at that time. Soon afterward a young preacher who told the story in another village was arrested and accused of spreading false rumors of superstition. As a part of his trial the case was fully investigated, and much to the surprise of the court, it was found to be totally true.

David Wang, general director of Asian Outreach, tells of a recent trip he made to Inner Mongolia. In one of the house church meetings he met a woman who had been deserted by her husband. She could no longer survive in her native village, so she took her son and went to another town, but could find no place to live. Finally the local president took them to a vacant house and gave them permission to stay there. A week later he asked them how they were getting on. He was surprised when they told him that all was well. Surprised, because he had somewhat mischievously assigned them to a haunted house, so notorious that no one even dared walk by it at night.

The atheist president was so deeply impressed that the demons had no power over this Christian woman he asked her if she would pray for a woman in the village who had been demon possessed for years. She was a hopeless case, kept chained to the floor, and so violent that her food had to be thrown to her like a wild beast. The Christian woman asked for time to prepare, went back to her native village and recruited a prayer team to come with her; they were taken by the president to the demonized woman's hut. A large crowd gathered outside. One of the prayer team soon came out and asked for water for bathing and for some clothes. In an hour the sick woman walked out, healed and in her right mind. Many people in that village believed in Jesus as a result of that demonstration of power evangelism.[16]

Power Evangelism in Argentina

For the better part of the twentieth century, the growth of evangelical churches in Argentina was very slow compared to the rest of Latin America. But this changed dramatically in 1982 when Argentina lost the Falkland Islands war to Great Britain. Previous to that, Argentines had gained a reputation of being the proudest of all Latin Americans. But losing the war, especially when their generals had lied to the people and told them they were winning, broke that pride and significantly altered the social psychology of the nation. No longer trusting their military, nor the traditional Catholic church, which had been aligned with the military, nor their government, Argentines were suddenly forced to look beyond themselves for something on which to anchor their lives.

God was ready for them. On the very day the battleship General Belgrano was sunk by the British, a young businessman in his late 30s named Carlos Annacondia launched his powerful public evangelistic ministry. Annacondia, the owner of a nuts and bolts factory, had been converted in 1979 under the ministry of Manuel Ruiz, a Latin American diplomat. Annacondia is now recognized as the foremost evangelist in Argentina. Still a layperson, he holds several crusades a year in Argentina's teeming urban areas. In each crusade he will typically preach each night for 30 or 40 nights to crowds of up to 40,000, standing in vacant lots from 8:00 P.M. to midnight and after. It is estimated that in his first five years of ministry over 1 million have made public decisions for Christ, which, by way of comparison, is roughly what Billy Graham saw in his first 20 years.

I recently spent some time with Carlos Annacondia in Argentina, and was deeply impressed by his combination of humility and power. The only kind of evangelism he knows is power evangelism. A prominent part of a typical service is a prolonged, public rebuke of the devil and all his forces. When he does this, words flow from his mouth in an eloquent torrent carried far and wide by a state-of-the-art public address system. Sometimes this rebuke will last for 15 or 20 minutes. Before he is through, demons brought in by people in the audience will begin to manifest dramatically, often throwing the individuals to the ground kicking and screaming. Well-trained teams of ushers will move through the crowd and escort (at times with no little force) the demonized to a huge, 150-foot yellow and white striped tent behind the platform. Annacondia calls this his "spiritual intensive care unit" where other teams of believers with the gift of exorcism exercise a deliverance ministry, some until dawn.

Meanwhile, as Annacondia preaches penetrating biblical gospel messages, hundreds of others are saved and healed. When the invitation for salvation is given, people literally run forward to the roped off area where they register their decisions for Christ with counselors seated at long tables. Almost every kind of miracle conceivable has been documented in Carlos Annacondia's *conquistas*, as he calls them, but the most frequent is the miraculous filling of teeth. In fact, only those who have had three or more teeth filled or replaced are allowed to give public testimony. One or two teeth are now considered somewhat trivial.

Dental miracles are also common in the ministry of Omar Cabrera, who, with his wife, Marfa, pastors the Vision of the Future Church. This church, with 145,000 members is the world's third largest behind Paul Yonggi Cho's Yoido Church in Korea (550,000) and Javier Vasquez' Jotabeche Church in Chile (over 300,000). When I was with Cabrera recently, I was skeptical enough of miraculous tooth filling for him to introduce me to one of his administrative assistants, a woman in her 50s named Ana whose teeth had been filled several years previously. While she had been a dentist's patient, she had skipped several years of visits until her teeth were badly decayed. Through Omar Cabrera's prayer, five molars were filled. She then did go to the dentist who confirmed they had been filled with a compound unknown to him, that was "hard as a diamond." When she told me she had not had a cavity since, I asked permission to look into her mouth. Sure enough, the teeth were smoothly filled with rows of a substance somewhat whiter than the teeth themselves.

While a few Argentine Christian leaders remain skeptical, power evangelism has become the norm. Pastor Norberto Carlini's Sanctuary of Faith Church in the city of Rosario grew from 500 to 5,000 in three years, and he has purchased three city blocks to construct his sanctuary. A former convict and drug addict when he was in his 20s, Hector Gimenez has seen his Church of the Miracles of Jesus Christ in Buenos Aires grow from nothing to over 20,000 in less than a year. They have leased a theater where he preaches four services a day, every day.

In the city of La Plata, Alberto Scataglini's Church of the Diagonal sponsored Carlos Annacondia's first city-wide crusade, and it has since grown from 500 to 2,500.

Rather unexpectedly, I participated in some power evangelism during my last visit to Argentina. After one of Omar Cabrera's nightly rallies in a sports arena in Cordoba where he preached to several thousand and saw many healed and saved, my friend Edgardo Silvoso, the director of Harvest Evangelism based in San Jose, California, took my wife and me out to dinner with several other friends from the States. Edgardo asked us to sit with some Chinese brothers and sisters, who were visiting from San Francisco, in order to help interpret for them what they were seeing. After asking many questions relating to whether signs and wonders were really for today, one of them mentioned that he had been suffering a terrible pain in his back. I asked him if he would like me to pray for healing; he agreed.

So we moved his chair away from the table toward the center of the restaurant, where I could pick up his feet and check his legs. One was shorter than the other, and it lengthened as I prayed. Then I laid hands on his back, prayed and the pain left. By then most of the others in our party had left their places at the table and gathered around, as did a couple of waiters. A young American missionary then asked for prayer. As I prayed, the Holy Spirit came with visible power, the man started weeping loudly and then began to confess his sins. By this time seven waiters had joined the group. One asked me to pray against some white spots on his head. I first lengthened his leg, then prayed against the spots, but this time with no immediate effect. Another waiter asked me to pray for his sprained thumb.

Edgardo Silvoso, who among other things is an evangelist, spoke up and called the seven waiters to gather around him. He explained to them what they were witnessing, and told them of God's power not only to heal them but to save them. Then he invited any of them who wished to accept Jesus Christ as Savior and Lord to put their hands in his and pray with him. All seven did, and suddenly another waiter came running up and shoved his hand in as well. Afterwards, we all embraced and rejoiced in the presence of God.

Power Evangelism at the Vineyard

Most of this chapter has reported exciting things that God is doing around the world, but not much has been said of the U.S. I recall not too long ago that one of my seminary professor colleagues became irritated at hearing such things, and said to me, "All the stories you missionaries tell happen out there where we can't check up on them to see whether they are true or false. Why doesn't it ever happen around here?" The answer, of course, is that it's happening around here as well.

In almost every one of the past few years either the

Assemblies of God or the Church of God (Cleveland, TN) has shown up as the fastest growing U.S. denomination. Although reliable figures are hard to come by, the Church of God in Christ might well be growing even more rapidly. All three, of course, are classical Pentecostal denominations. When independent charismatic churches are combined with classical Pentecostals, the current U.S. decadal growth rate is 173 percent, many times higher than any similar grouping including sects such as Mormons or Jehovah's Witnesses.[17]

Elmer Towns recently compiled a list of the fastest growing local churches in each of the 50 states for *Ministries Today* (Sept.-Oct. 1986) and found that 40 of the 50 were Pentecostal or charismatic. *Christianity Today* chronicled the phenomenon by devoting its October 16, 1987 issue to "America's Pentecostals: Who They Are; What They Believe; Where They Are Going."

As a sub-group the independent charismatics have been the fastest growing religious group in America in the decade of the '80s. One of the leaders among them has been Vineyard Christian Fellowship in Anaheim, California. My skeptical professor friend could have seen what missionaries see if he had been willing to take a drive of less than an hour from the seminary.

In the last chapter I described my relationship with John Wimber and his ministry at Fuller Seminary. The reason his teaching there was so powerful was chiefly because everything he said was backed with front-line ministry.

The phrase *power evangelism* in the title of this chapter and in frequent references throughout the book was coined by John Wimber to help describe what he saw God doing in the Vineyard. He defines and describes power evangelism and shows how it relates to the ministry of Vineyard Christian Fellowship in his twin books *Power Evangelism* and *Power Healing*. Wimber says, "By power evangelism I mean a presentation of the gospel that is rational, but that also transcends the rational. The explanation of the gospel comes with a demonstration of God's power through signs and wonders." It has worked so well in his experience because, "In power evangelism, resistance to the gospel is overcome by the demonstration of God's power in supernatural events, and receptivity to Christ's claims is usually very high."[18]

As we move from the twentieth to the twenty-first century we find ourselves in an age of the expansion of the kingdom of God unmatched throughout Christian history.

Not only has the Anaheim Vineyard grown to around 6,000 largely through power evangelism, but John Wimber has a vision for establishing no less than 10,000 Vineyard Fellowships throughout North America by A.D. 2000. Currently they report 250, and their young denomination is known as the Association of Vineyard Churches. Their quarterly newsletter regularly carries a column entitled, "Works of the Father," in which cases of miraculous healing as a result of the ministry of these churches are documented. I have no doubt that my professor friend would be surprised to know that here in the United States:

—Joe, 4, from the San Fernando Valley was born with strabismus (crossed eyes), which the doctor had declared irreversible and scheduled an operation. He received two months of prayer therapy, and was found to be completely normal at the pre-op examination.

—In St. Louis, Jackie Berry, 16, saw her back healed of scoliosis through prayer.

—Laura of Shreveport, Louisiana had inoperable cancer of the liver and was given three to six months to live. After seven months of prayer therapy tests showed no cancer at all.

—Warren of San Jose, California had been deaf in one ear since the Korean War. He received prayer and his hearing returned immediately.

—In Evanston, Illinois a team prayed for a woman blind in one eye due to an accident. Laser surgery had removed over 50 tumors and the retina and lens had deteriorated. In 15 minutes her sight returned and doctors in the Mayo Clinic could not find so much as any scars from the operations.

—Doctors had given up on Rachel, 1, whose kidneys failed due to a rare virus. Prayer was offered at the morning service of the Vineyard in Santa Clara Valley, California, and by 1:00 that afternoon, her kidneys began to function. In a few days she had no more trace of the disease.[19]

WHAT THE SPIRIT IS SAYING

A chapter like this could hardly have been written at the beginning of our twentieth century. Some of what has been described was occurring at mid-century, but not much. However, as we move from the twentieth to the twenty-first century we find ourselves in an age of the expansion of the kingdom of God unmatched throughout Christian history.

Among the many things that God is doing in the world today is using His people as instruments for power evangelism. I happen to believe that through it the Holy Spirit is saying something extremely important to the churches. Many who have an ear to hear are learning to participate in this work of the Spirit through the first wave of the Pentecostal movement and through the second wave of the charismatic movement. Others are responding to the call of the Spirit through the third wave.

Regardless of the form it takes, they are saying, "Yes, Holy Spirit, I hear what you are saying to the churches. I like what you are doing. Please count me in."

Notes _____

1. Kevin Perrotta, "A Third Wave," *New Covenant*, Dec. 1983, p. 19.
2. Rufus Anderson, "Principles and Methods of Modern Missions," (1869) in *Classics of Christian Missions*, Francis M. DuBose, ed.,(Nashville, TN: Broadman Press, 1979), p. 254.
3. Patrick Johnstone, *Operation World*, (Pasadena, CA: William Carey Library, 1986), p. 35.
4. Sharon E. Mumper, "Where in the World Is the Church Growing?" *Christianity Today*, July 11, 1986, p. 17.
5. C. Peter Wagner, "Church Growth," *Dictionary of the Pentecostal and Charismatic Movements*, Stanley M. Burgess and Gary B. McGee, eds., (Grand Rapids: Zondervan Publishing House, 1988).
6. For faith projections of the Central American Church, see Emilio Antonio Nuñez, ed., *La Hora de Dios para Guatemala*, (Guatemala City: SEPAL, 1983), p. 177.
7. These testimonies are taken from *Miracles and Healing*, a newsletter published by the Deeper Life Church in Lagos, Nigeria, Vol. 1, Nos. 7 and 9, n.d.
8. Ibid.
9. John N. Vaughan, *The World's Twenty Largest Churches*, (Grand Rapids, MI: Baker Book House, 1984), p. 211.
10. Ramsay MacMullen, *Christianizing the Roman Empire, A.D. 100-400* (New Haven, CT: Yale University Press, 1984), p. 27.
11. Paul Eshleman, *I Just Saw Jesus*, (San Bernardino, CA: Here's Life Publishers, 1985), pp. 114-115.

12. Ibid., pp. 105,106.
13. Ibid., pp. 111,112.
14. Ibid., pp. 110,111.
15. Among the best of the new books on the growth of the church in China are *China the Emerging Challenge* by Paul E. Kauffman (Grand Rapids, MI:Baker Book House, 1982), *The Church in China* by Carl Lawrence (Minneapolis, MI:Bethany House Publishers, 1985), *God Reigns in China* by Leslie Lyall (London:Hodder and Stoughton, 1985), *China: The Church's Long March* by David H. Adeney (Ventura, CA: Regal Books, Div. of Gospel Light Publications, 1985) and *China Miracle* by Arthur Wallis (Colombia, MO: City Hill Publishing, 1986).
16. C. Peter Wagner, ed., *Signs and Wonders Today*, (Altamonte Springs, FL: Creation House), 1987, pp. 83-84.
17. Wagner, *Dictionary*.
18. John Wimber with Kevin Springer, *Power Evangelism*, (San Francisco: Harper & Row, 1986), p. 35.
19. *The Vineyard Newsletter*, Spring 1986; Fall/Winter 1986; Spring 1987.

FOUR

LIVING THE LIFE-STYLE OF THE KINGDOM

I t is one thing to hear about the wondrous works of God in the world, and even to get excited about them. But it is something else to raise the question as to whether such things *should* be happening. To put it another way, most sincere Christians want to know sooner or later if what they are experiencing actually fits with what the Bible teaches.

Theological issues regarding the ministry of healing are particularly high on the agendas of Christian leaders who come from traditional evangelical backgrounds, as I explained in chapter 1. Where the teachings of Benjamin Warfield, John MacArthur, Jr., C. I. Scofield or any numbers of others have been prominent, the shift into the third wave is not that easy. Not only pastors, but Christian lay leaders as well would be irresponsible if they attempted to begin a healing ministry in their local church without first asking the tough theological questions. Skirting the issues carries a high risk of making your church sick, and that is exactly what this book is trying to avoid.

I wish I could develop a theology with which every Christian would agree. But this is impossible. Many have tried through the ages, and no one has succeeded. I will attempt, however, to suggest a theological framework in which to understand third-wave ministries, a framework intended to be compatible with the basics of traditional evangelical theology and one that I hope will offend as few evangelicals as possible.

STARTING WITH THE KINGDOM

My starting point is not original. I clearly recall that as I was sitting under the teaching of John Wimber in the early '80s, he began talking about a theology of the kingdom of God in a way that made a good bit of sense. In fact, the first chapter in his book *Power Evangelism* is titled, "The Kingdom of God." Nor does Wimber claim originality. He says, "Much of this chapter is based on material gleaned from the writings of George Ladd and James Kallas."[1]

Many others have agreed with Wimber that the kingdom of God provides a helpful starting point for understanding the work of God today. Ken Blue, for example, has published a new book, *Authority to Heal*, which I personally recommend as the best current third-wave theology. His Part II deals with "The Kingdom of God and the Fight to Heal."[2]

Most every Christian has memorized the Lord's

Prayer, which includes the line, "Thy kingdom come, Thy will be done on earth as it is in heaven" (Matt. 6:10, *RSV*). I knew the Lord's Prayer even before I became a Christian. In fact, it is so familiar that many Christians recite it over and over without even stopping to think what the words really mean. I did this for years. And then when I finally did stop and ask myself what I meant by "Thy kingdom come, Thy will be done on earth as it is in heaven," I discovered that I had been making two rather subtle assumptions.

First, I assumed that the kingdom was future. My prayer, in effect, was requesting that Jesus would come the second time. I had been taught that the church age had been ushered in at Pentecost and that the kingdom of God was put on hold until Jesus returned. I did not doubt that miracles had happened in the past and that they would happen in the future. But today? Well, we now have science and medicine and computers and, above all, the Bible, which is the written Word of God. With all that, I thought, why look for miracles?

Second, I assumed that in the present God's will was, in fact, being done on earth. Since God is absolutely sovereign, whatever happens on earth must be approved by Him. When I prayed for a sick person, I would frequently say, "God, please give her the grace to endure this illness and comfort her family." The unspoken implication was that when we're sick, it is ordinarily God's will that we be sick, so we endure the best we can.

A key part of opening myself to understanding the third wave was taking another look at these two assumptions. As I did, I began to realize that they are both true, but incomplete. Yes, God's kingdom is future, but it is also present. Yes, God is sovereign, but Satan is also active in the world today, and he works forcefully against God's will. Therefore, some things we see happening could be caused by Satan and not by God. I sang about this every time I sang Martin Luther's "A Mighty Fortress," but I was blind to its major implications. Luther said: "For still our ancient foe does seek to work us woe. His craft and power are great, and, armed with cruel hate, on earth is not his equal."

What, then, are the implications, especially for developing an effective healing ministry?

"Thy Kingdom Come"

When we pray, "Thy kingdom come," what exactly does this mean?

A fundamental premise for understanding this is the biblical teaching that Satan is "the god of this age" (2 Cor. 4:4). In some sense of the words, Satan is in control of the world as we know it. The world is Satan's kingdom, and it has been since Adam and Eve gave up their control by disobeying God.

To some this sounds as if I have gone overboard and assigned too much power to Satan. But I don't think so if we take seriously the dialogue between Jesus and Satan in Jesus' temptation. At one point Satan took Jesus on a high mountain and showed Him the kingdoms of the world. Then he said, "All these things I will give You if You will fall down and worship me" (Matt 4:9). Was Satan playing games with Jesus, or was this for real? For one thing, Jesus did not question whether Satan had the right to give away the kingdoms, so apparently he did. For another, when Luke describes the same scenario, he quotes Satan as saying, "This has been delivered to me, and I give it to whomever I wish" (Luke 4:6). The theme is later picked up by John, who says, "The whole world lies under the sway of the wicked one" (1 John 5:19).

While all this is true, it is also true that Satan is not the ultimate owner of this world. "The earth is the Lord's, and all its fullness, the world and those who dwell therein" (Ps. 24:1). God is the King of kings and the Lord of lords. Satan is a usurper. He has taken what is not his own. But make no mistake about it, he has taken it. How much power he might have on other planets and on other galaxies we do not know. But we do know "on earth is not his equal," as Martin Luther affirms. It is temporary, but his power is nevertheless awesome.

Satan's power is dramatized by a story coming out of Tibet, where the forces of evil have gone virtually unchallenged through the ages. Paul Kauffman, president of Asian Outreach, picked up a revealing news report from the July 16, 1982 *Far East Economic Review.* It seems that an Australian acupuncturist was asked to treat an old Tibetan exile, then living in India. To his amazement, none of the needles could penetrate the Tibetan's skin. The acupuncturist apologized profusely and said such a thing had never happened to him before.

"Oh," said the Tibetan, "it is I who am sorry. I forgot to take my amulet off." When he removed the charm from his neck, the needles went in easily. Then he explained: "A Lama gave me the amulet to protect me against the bullets of the Chinese."[3] This is what I mean when I say that Satan has awesome power.

When we realize that Satan has usurped so much control, it serves to dramatize all the more the significance of Jesus' coming to earth, because Jesus brought with Him a new kingdom. This was nothing less than an invasion of hostile territory and a clash of mighty powers. Jesus' kingdom has engaged Satan's kingdom in battle. I see now that every healing of Jesus was an act of war, an embarrassment to Satan. Every demon cast out was an insult to Satan.

It is so clear to me now that the kingdom of God is present as well as future that I wonder how I missed it for so long.

Bible teachers have pointed out that Jesus came to earth for many reasons. But among them, this one is very clear: "For this purpose the Son of God was manifested, that He might destroy the works of the devil" (1 John 3:8).

How Could I Miss It?

It is so clear to me now that the kingdom of God is present as well as future that I wonder how I missed it for so long. When I took my theological studies at Fuller Seminary back in the early '50s, George Ladd was one of my professors. He was well on his way, even then, to becoming one of the nation's experts on the biblical theology of the kingdom of God. But I was so fascinated by dispensationalism and the Scofield Bible at that time that I wasn't hearing what he was saying. I am now embarrassed to admit that what I most remember about George Ladd was his irreverent questioning of the pretribulation rapture, considered evangelical iconoclasm by many in those days.

During my ministry in Bolivia as a missionary, I continued to assume that the kingdom was on hold. But then when I joined the Fuller School of World Mission faculty in 1971, I began to notice that my colleague Arthur Glasser was talking about the kingdom of God a great deal, and I slowly began to catch on. I finally realized how ignorant of the subject I was when my friend Raymond J. Bakke of Northern Baptist Seminary reviewed one of my books and said, "It's been a long time since I read a significant work on ecclesiology or missiology that never once mentioned the kingdom."[4] I learned my lesson then and there, and went back to George Ladd's books. Ladd asserts that "Modern scholarship is quite unanimous in the opinion that the kingdom of God was the central message of Jesus."[5]

What Ladd teaches is that the Bible sees two major phases of human history, referred to as the present age and the age to come. Up to the time of Jesus' first coming, the present age was here by itself, and Satan was largely in control. But Jesus' coming, climaxed by His death and resurrection, introduced the age to come, the kingdom of God present now on the earth. At Jesus' second coming the present age will be terminated, Satan will be thrown into the lake of fire, and the age to come, called the new heaven and new earth, will prevail forever. Right now, between Jesus' two comings, we are involved in a war.

I now believe that the kingdom of God should be much more central to our preaching than the evangelical community has tended to make it. John the Baptist said, "The kingdom of heaven is at hand!" (Matt. 3:2). Jesus proclaimed "The kingdom of heaven is at hand" (4:17). The apostles were sent out to preach, "The kingdom of heaven is at hand" (10:7). Acts begins with Jesus teaching on the kingdom of God (see Acts 1:3) and ends with Paul preaching on it (see 28:31).

We do well to keep in mind that there is a qualitative

difference between what we see happening in the Old Testament days and what we see happening now. Of course, even through the Old Testament we see that Jehovah God was King of kings and Lord of lords. His mighty power intervened on behalf of His people. How else could we understand the Flood or the Exodus or Elijah on Mount Carmel or Daniel in the lions den? Still, when Jesus came, the kingdom of God was introduced into human history in a way that it never had been previously. George Ladd points out that a crucial turning point in history occurred when Jesus said, "I saw Satan fall like lightning from heaven" (Luke 10:18).

After that incident, Jesus told His disciples that they were particularly privileged to see the things they were seeing. He added, "for I tell you that many prophets and kings have desired to see what you see, and have not seen it" (v. 24), contrasting Old Testament figures with them. On another occasion He said that while there was no greater prophet than John the Baptist, even the least in the kingdom of God is greater than he (see 7:28).

Satan had enormous power until Jesus came. But the cross of Jesus Christ has broken that power. Scripture teaches that on the cross, Jesus disarmed principalities and powers and made a public spectacle of them (see Col. 2:15). If this is true, why does Satan continue to exercise power? It is because in this interim period, which some call the "already and the not yet," Satan is like a lion that has taken a load of buckshot, but has not yet died. This makes the enemy more ferocious than ever, more destructive and even more powerful through rage.

While passages in the book of Revelation have traditionally been subject to various interpretations, one at least illustrates what I am saying here. Revelation 12:9

says that Satan was cast out of heaven. Then it warns the people on earth to watch out, since "the devil has come down to you, having great wrath, because he knows that he has a short time" (v. 12). I recall that Paul Yonggi Cho once mentioned that Korea was formally liberated from their Japanese oppressors on August 15, 1945, but over the next several months Japanese con-

The kingdom of God is a reign, not a realm. The citizens of the kingdom are those people who willfully submit themselves to Jesus as their King.

tinued to kill Koreans until the liberation became functional. So we live in a period like that where Satan is ultimately defeated, but he's plenty mad about it, and bent on doing all the damage he can.

"Thy Will Be Done on Earth as It Is in Heaven"

In the Lord's Prayer, as soon as we pray, "Thy kingdom come," we go on to pray, "Thy will be done on earth as it is in heaven." This begins to give us some indication of what our ministry is to be. It helps us understand what God wants to do through us in this time of warfare between the kingdom of Satan and the kingdom of God.

We must realize that God's kingdom is not some geographical territory with political boundaries. Jesus affirmed time and again that "My kingdom is not of this world" (John 18:36). The kingdom of God is a reign, not a realm. The citizens of the kingdom are those people who willfully submit themselves to Jesus as their King. If you are one such person, the kingdom of God is present wherever you go. That's why Jesus said that "the kingdom of God is within you" (Luke 17:21). Where God's will is being done on earth as it is in heaven, there you find the kingdom of God.

But what does this kingdom look like? What are its chief characteristics? What are some of the signs that will let us know for sure if the kingdom is really here?

THE SIGNS OF THE KINGDOM

A helpful approach for understanding this is to inquire as to what is going on in heaven. We don't know everything about it, but the Bible does give us some fairly clear indications. What happens when God is in charge and the devil is totally eliminated from the picture? We see some of that in the Garden of Eden before Adam and Eve fell into sin. And we see more in the New Jerusalem after the devil is cast into the lake of fire. In the New Jerusalem "there shall be no more death, nor sorrow, nor crying; and there shall be no more pain" (Rev. 21:4).

Let's be specific now. I have chosen six out of who-knows-how-many characteristics common to both the original creation and the New Jerusalem, which will be helpful as we attempt to understand the ministry of the kingdom.

In the kingdom of God:

1. There are no poor.

2. There is no war.

3. There are no oppressed people.

4. No one is demonized.

5. No one is sick.

6. No one is lost.

To put it another way, all of the above—poverty, war, oppression, demonization, sickness and being lost—are works of Satan, which entered the human race at the time of the Fall and have been here ever since.

So, when we pray, "Thy will be done on earth as it is in heaven," we are asking God to use us as representatives of the kingdom to the greatest extent possible to see that where there is war now, there be peace, or where there is oppression, there be liberation. For instance, Jesus said, "But if I cast out demons with the finger of God, surely the kingdom of God has come upon you" (Luke 11:20). People here on earth are demonized, because it remains the kingdom of Satan. But when God's kingdom invades, demons are defeated.

When Jesus first began His ministry, He wanted to be sure His followers had a clear picture of the ministry of the kingdom He was bringing to earth. So He went into the synagogue in His hometown of Nazareth and, reading from Isaiah 61, declared that He had come to proclaim good news to the poor, heal the brokenhearted, deliver the captives, give sight to the blind and liberate the oppressed (see Luke 4:18).

Another list of the signs of the kingdom appears toward the end of the Gospel of Mark, where Jesus sends out His apostles to preach the gospel to every creature and says, "These signs will follow those who believe" (16:17). He mentions driving out demons, speaking in other tongues, taking up serpents, drinking poison and healing the sick through laying on of hands (see Mark 16:15-18).

I realize that some biblical scholars debate whether these were authentic words of Jesus or whether they might have been added by some editor in the second century. True, the Mark 16:9-20 passage is not to be found in the ancient Codex Sinaiticus or Codex Vaticanus manuscripts. But I agree with Michael Harper, who says, "In my opinion the authorship is not important. Every word of the passage is consistent with the Acts of the apostles, and so can be accepted whoever the author was."[6]

Not only are such signs found in the Acts of the apostles, but they are seen in real life today. While in eastern Bolivia, my wife, Doris, and I had to make a day's horseback trip through the jungle to visit some missionaries who worked among Ayore Indians at a place called Bella Vista. It was so isolated that we were the first missionaries who had ever visited them. We set off with our daughter Karen, 4, and soon were shocked to realize that we had neglected to bring canteens of water with us. The climate was very hot and very dry, and we had a ride of several hours ahead of us, but we decided that rather than turn back we would see what water we could find on the way. Sure enough, we found sizable pools of water here and there along the trail, and quenched our thirst.

The surprise came when we arrived, and John and Phoebe Depue noticed that we had no canteens. "What did you drink?" they asked with some dismay. We told them we drank out of the pools, and they almost collapsed. "Oh, no!" they exclaimed. "The Ayores went through the other day and poisoned all those pools to get the fish out. That's deadly poison!" But we felt no ill effects and rejoiced that, while scholars may argue, the power of God is real today.

Similar things are happening, not only with poison, but also with snakes. Eloise Clarno reports that in the Philippines recently Pastor Elmer Arrozena had prepared a sermon on Mark 16:15-18, but the church service had to be canceled because of a typhoon. That night a deadly cobra, driven by the storm, slithered under their door and was approaching his child. Through a reflex action, Arrozena grabbed the snake, and it bit him twice. One bite was enough to kill, never mind two. He lost consciousness, but his wife, Shirley, gathered some other Christians and fervently prayed. After 30 minutes, Pastor Arrozena came to in perfect health. The next Sunday he could preach with conviction: "They will take up serpents . . . it will by no means hurt them" (Mark 16:18).[7]

One of the clearest lists of the signs of the kingdom was given by Jesus to the disciples of John the Baptist. After John had been imprisoned, he became discouraged and wondered if what he had been preaching was the right gospel after all. So he sent his disciples to ask Jesus if He was really the one. Jesus responded by listing some of the public manifestations of His ministry: the blind see, the lame walk, lepers are cleansed, deaf hear, dead are raised and good news is preached to the poor (see Luke 7:22).

SIGNS IN FULLER SEMINARY

Just as with the signs that involve poison and snakes, we

are also seeing God make the lame walk and the blind receive their sight, the latter even closer to home in our classrooms at Fuller Seminary. Recently when I began one of my basic church growth classes and asked the students to introduce themselves, I had the privilege of meeting missionary Sam Sasser, who had served for many years with the Assemblies of God in the islands of the South Pacific. It was a large room, and he was sitting in the back in a wheelchair with his right foot wrapped in a thick bandage. I learned that he had survived several accidents including two in boats and a plane crash, and had to walk long distances on sharp coral reefs. As a result, he had contracted coral poisoning. His bone structure had been deteriorating from the effect of the poison, and he had undergone a number of surgeries over the past four years to remove decayed bone tissue. He did not know how long he would have to remain in a wheelchair.

On the second day of class, I began my regular routine of beginning each session with 20-30 minutes of prayer. I called on David Ellis, a missionary with the World Gospel Mission in Bolivia, to be our prayer leader that day, and asked for requests from the class. Sam Sasser requested prayer for healing. I suggested to Ellis that when he came to Sasser's name on the list he give an opportunity for several students around him to lay hands on before he prayed. So he did.

On the third day during the prayer time, Sam Sasser said he wanted to give a testimony. "I don't go for theatrics," he said, "but yesterday I didn't mention that I was also legally blind as a result of the coral poisoning. The first day I did not see you as you taught the class." (I had not paid much attention to the fact that his secretary, who had also pushed his wheelchair, was taking notes for him.) He continued, "After prayer yesterday, I could see you through the whole class. Not only that, but this morning the nurse came to change the bandage on my foot, and she couldn't believe what she saw. She told me that if whatever had started were to continue, I would be well in a week."

On the fourth day he raised his hand again. "The nurse told my doctor what she saw," he said, "so he called me in to his office this morning. When he took the bandage off, he laughed out loud. A large incision three inches long and one inch deep had completely healed over with a small scab on the top. He said, 'This can't happen. There's something wrong. I'm afraid there will be a pocket of infection inside.' So he opened the incision again to probe it with a Q-tip, but found nothing. He sent me today to be measured for special shoes."

Within another week, Sam Sasser was walking around the campus, pushing his own wheelchair. He canceled his enrollment in a special school to train him to use seeing eye dogs. While Sam is not yet able to play tennis or to read, and signs of the underlying coral poisoning flare up from time to time, God has been greatly glorified, and many in the seminary community have been encouraged by seeing these signs of the kingdom in our midst.

THE LIFE-STYLE OF THE KINGDOM

The net result of understanding the signs of the kingdom is to provide us with guidelines for the kinds of ministries we can expect God to lead us into if He answers our prayer, "Thy will be done on earth as it is in heaven." With them we develop a clearer picture of what the life-style of the kingdom is all about. As individuals, but even more importantly as active members of churches and other groupings of Christians, these kingdom ministries should be flowing through us on a regular basis. We should be concerned about the poor and oppressed. We should provide food for the hungry here in our own nation and around the world. We should seek to change social structures that create degrading conditions for fellow human beings, such as apartheid in South Africa or the caste system in India.

It is clear that kingdom theology, as we have been explaining it here, provides a sound rationale for social ministries of all kinds as well as for evangelism. Obviously, all the signs of the kingdom are important and should demand our attention. Prominent among them are healing the sick and casting out demons. Therefore, starting a healing ministry in your church could be seen as a natural result of the presence of Jesus and His kingdom. Many Christians, however, get nervous at this point. Sending medical supplies to earthquake victims in Mexico, supporting a Billy Graham crusade or signing a petition to free the Jews in the Soviet Union are much more comfortable activities than holding a healing service. Some, partly in self-defense, ask me if I believe signs and wonders are normative.

I think the answer to that depends on what *normative* means. I don't believe that supernatural signs and wonders are necessarily a sign of true Christianity, true spirituality or the true church. They are not listed under the fruit of the Spirit. Many notable Christians get along very well without them.

In my opinion, signs and wonders should be considered about as normative in Christianity as believer's baptism. Some, such as Baptists, Mennonites and Church of Christ, argue that you cannot have a true church without it. Others, such as Presbyterians, Episcopalians and Lutherans, think they have true churches without it. I happen to believe in it and require it of my family and anyone else whom I can influence, but I belong to a Congregational church in which it's OK if you do and just as OK if you don't. I see ministry in healing the sick and casting out demons in a similar light. I believe in it, I do it and I help as many others enter into that ministry as possible. But if some other Christian brothers and sisters see things differently, far be it from me to classify them, on those grounds, as second-class Christians.

THE PROBLEM OF THE LOST

One of the major purposes of this book is to help Christian people and Christian churches enter into a regular, effective healing ministry. It is necessary at times to remove roadblocks so this can happen. I have found that it is helpful for evangelicals to observe significant parallels between our kingdom ministry in reaching the lost and our kingdom ministry in healing the sick. Traditionally, among evangelicals, evangelism has been a higher agenda item than either social action, which liberals emphasize, or exorcising demons, which charismatics emphasize. Soteriology has been a stronger emphasis than social ethics or pneumatology.

Among evangelicals there is a consensus that God's will for reaching the lost is explicit in Scripture. Few question that He is "not willing that any should perish but that all should come to repentance" (2 Pet. 3:9). But while He wants all people to be saved, not all are.

Why is it, then, that God's will is not done and that many people He wants to be saved are not? Many different reasons could be given for individual cases, but the general answer is that keeping people lost is a direct act of Satan. The Scriptures teach this clearly. The apostle Paul says that if the gospel is veiled, it is veiled to those who are lost "whose minds the god of this age has blinded, who do not believe, lest the light of the gospel of the glory of Christ, who is the image of God, should shine on them" (2 Cor. 4:4). Evangelizing and getting people saved is a part of the kingdom warfare we have been describing. When a person is saved, it's a victory over the enemy. That's why we are told that the angels in heaven rejoice when it happens (see Luke 15:10).

We evangelicals have long since come to terms with the cold, clear fact that lostness is a reality and that it will continue to be a reality in our world until Jesus returns. Through the ages theologians have attempted to explain why. Volumes have been written on predestination and supralapsarianism and pre-soteric synergism, but no one has solved the problem to the satisfaction of all. Historic church councils have succeeded in explaining the Trinity and the relationship of the two natures of Christ, but they haven't explained this one.

But does all this worry people like Billy Graham or Bill Bright or Luis Palau? Not in the least. While theologians are trying to figure out why it does or does not happen, they keep preaching the gospel and getting as many saved as they possibly can. And most other evangelicals gladly join them.

THE PROBLEM OF THE SICK

But while the issues are almost identical, the reaction to them is not, when it comes to healing the sick. Many evangelicals will stumble at the realization that not every one we pray for is healed. A typical approach is that taken by one of my fellow professors in Fuller Seminary, who was particularly disturbed that John Wimber and I were teaching our MC510 course in the seminary and that rumors were circulating that people in the course were actually being healed right on campus. He was quoted anonymously in *Christianity Today* as criticizing us for teaching a "lottery Christianity in which there must be a few big winners—spectacular healings—and many $10 winners—cured headaches—in order to attract a crowd." His major objection was that such teaching is far from a theology of the cross.[8]

I don't pretend to have a final answer for why some people are not healed any more than I have one for why some people are not saved. But let's think about it a bit.

First of all, is sickness God's will? A good way to address that question is to raise another one. Is sickness a kingdom value? Obviously not. As we have seen, it is as contrary to the life-style of the kingdom of God as is poverty or war.

If sickness is not God's will, but many people in fact are sick, what is the cause? The answer clearly is Satan. I agree with Robert Wise, who says, "Let's mark the conclusion in red letters. The disasters of the world do not have their origin in the will of God. The evil one is the author of adversity."[9]

I believe that Satan works in three major ways to bring sickness and suffering on people:

1. Satan causes sickness directly. An obvious tactic is demonization. For example, approximately 25 percent of Jesus' healings as recorded in the Gospel of Mark involve demons. The direct influence of the devil is explicitly demonstrated when Jesus healed a crippled woman and was scolded by a synagogue leader for doing it on the Sabbath. Jesus said, "Ought not this woman, being a daughter of Abraham, whom Satan has bound—think of it—for eighteen years, be loosed from this bond on the Sabbath?" (Luke 13:16). Satan's direct role is also explicit in the case of Job. What percentage of sickness is directly caused by Satan we do not know, but unquestionably much is.

2. Satan indirectly uses the natural results of the Fall to cause sickness and suffering. He uses bacteria, viruses, malnutrition, accidents, fights, poison, old age, rapists, murderers and on and on. In all probability most sickness falls into this category.

3. Satan tempts people to fall into sin, and God at times uses sickness to punish them for it. There are many examples in the Old Testament of plagues, which God sent on His own people to punish them for sin. When some Israelites rebelled against Moses and Aaron, God sent a plague and killed 14,700 (see Num. 16:45-50). Then God killed another 50,070 Israelites at Beth Shemesh when they disobeyed him by looking into the ark of the Lord (see 1 Sam. 6:19), just to cite two examples. In the New Testament, God made Elymas the sorcerer blind as part of a power encounter (see Acts 13:6-12). In Corinth some believers were sick and some had died as a result of abusing the Lord's supper (see 1 Cor. 11:30).

No matter what the immediate cause, the usual outcomes of sickness are pain, suffering and death, all the works of Satan.

But despite the intentions of Satan, some of the net results of sickness can be beneficial. We are told that in all things God works for the good of those who love him (see Rom. 8:28). People like Joni Eareckson Tada testify from their wheelchair that God has used their disease to minister His love to many. She says, "Satan schemed that a 17-year-old girl named Joni would break her neck, hoping to ruin her life; God sent the broken neck in answer to her prayer for a closer walk with Him and uses her wheelchair as a platform to display His sustaining grace."[10]

My late colleague on the Fuller Seminary faculty Tom Brewster was a quadriplegic throughout his whole adult life. He did not like his handicap, nor did he believe it had come from God. We prayed with him until the day he died that God would heal him. Nevertheless, he frequently said that God used His diving injury to teach him things and to mold his life in ways that would seem to have been impossible without it.

Even the apostle Paul experienced the blessing of God on his life through his "thorn in the flesh." Some argue that this wasn't a physical affliction, but whatever it might have been, it clearly was a message directly from Satan, and Paul didn't like it one bit. He prayed three times to get rid of it, but it didn't go. Through it all, Paul realized that God was using it to keep him humble, and for that he was glad. He said, "I take pleasure in infirmities" (see 2 Cor. 12:7-10).

REJOICING IN THE POWER

Both sickness and lostness will be with us until Jesus comes. Why they continue when we know they are not the will of God is one of those puzzling questions the Bible simply does not answer for us. If someone comes up with the answer, I'm sure he or she will be a candidate for a Nobel prize in theology.

Meanwhile, I am willing to live with it. And I continue to pray daily, "Thy will be done on earth as it is in heaven." Because I am a front-line representative of the kingdom of God, I will continue to oppose the works of Satan. In the power of the Holy Spirit I will witness to the lost and pray for the sick, knowing ahead of time that not all will be saved and not all will be healed. But some will, and that constitutes abundant reward for labors invested. That is where I will rejoice, and join the angels of heaven in so doing.

Notes _____

1. John Wimber with Kevin Springer, *Power Evangelism* (San Francisco: Harper & Row, 1986), pp. 186,187.
2. Ken Blue, *Authority to Heal* (Downer's Grove, IL: InterVarsity Press, 1987), p. 65.
3. Paul E. Kauffman, "Another Look at Tibet," *Asian Report*. No. 138, Jan. 1983, p. 9.
4. Raymond J. Bakke, "Our Kind of People," *Evangelical Missions Quarterly*, Apr. 1980, p. 127.
5. George Eldon Ladd, *A Theology of the New Testament* (Grand Rapids, MI: Wm. B. Eerdmans Pub. Co., 1974), p. 57.
6. Michael Harper, *The Healings of Jesus* (Downers Grove, IL: InterVarsity Press, 1986), p. 163.
7. See *Foursquare World Advance*, July/Aug. 1983, p. 11.
8. Tim Stafford, "Testing the Wine from John Wimber's Vineyard," *Christianity Today*, Aug. 8, 1986, p. 21.
9. Robert L. Wise, *When There Is No Miracle* (Ventura, CA: Regal Books, Div. of Gospel Light Publications, 1977), p. 128.
10. Joni Eareckson Tada and Steve Estes, *A Step Further* (Grand Rapids, MI: Zondervan Publishing House, 1978), p. 140.

FIVE

PASSING THE POWER

One of Jesus' most astounding statements was made to His apostles toward the end of His ministry: "Most assuredly, I say to you, he who believes in Me, the works that I do he will do also; and greater works than these he will do, because I go to My Father" (John 14:12).

How are we to understand this?

When I went to seminary, I was taught not to take it literally. That was the evangelical party line at the time. Many still teach it. Ray Stedman, for example, asks what greater works than physical healing could be done? He answers, "Why, *spiritual* healings. God wants most of all to heal the hurt in man's *spirit*." One reason Stedman stresses this is that he feels "It is always a mistake to put great emphasis on a physical miracle. Although miracles attract attention, they also tend to confuse people, so that ultimately the observers miss the point of what God is saying."[1] This undoubtedly is the most widely accepted interpretation among American Christians today.

Of course, Pentecostals and charismatics take Jesus' words literally. And I believe that evangelicals moving into the third wave should not be afraid to take them literally as well. I agree with Michael Harper, who says, "The early Christians claimed to possess that same power which Christ had manifested, particularly in his healing work." And how did they get it? "Jesus passed on . . . the same gifts of the Holy Spirit."[2]

The obvious key to this is accurately understanding the work of the Holy Spirit. Notice that Jesus said the power He was talking about would come "because I go to my Father." What is significant about that? Jesus later said, "If I do not go away, the Helper will not come to you; but if I depart, I will send Him to you" (John 16:7). The Helper, of course, is the Holy Spirit. This leads me to the theological hypothesis of this chapter: *The Holy Spirit was the source of all of Jesus' power during His earthly ministry. Jesus exercised no power of or by Himself. We today can expect to do the same or greater things than Jesus did because we have been given access to the same power source.*

JESUS' TWO NATURES

Classical Christian theology teaches that Jesus Christ had two natures, a divine nature and a human nature. This does not mean that He was two persons, but one person with two natures. Nor was He half-God and half-human, like some creatures in Greek mythology. Amazingly enough, He was 100-percent God and 100-percent human. Mathematically that may not seem to work out, but biblically and theologically it does. The ancient Latin phrase theologians toss around is: *vere deus et vere homo,* totally God and totally human.

I stress this because I do not want to be misunderstood. For me the classical doctrine of the two natures of Christ is a theological non-negotiable. Nothing I say in the next few pages should be interpreted to compromise in the least the fact that Jesus was truly God and truly human. The issues I am going to raise do not question whether Jesus had two natures, but rather how the two natures He did have related to one another.

DID JESUS REALLY KNOW?

An interesting starting point for this is what I think of as the problem of Mark 13:32. Here is Jesus on the Mount of Olives talking privately to Peter, James, John and Andrew. They ask Him when the end will come. Jesus tells them of many things that will happen in the end times, such as wars and rumors of wars and earthquakes and persecution and false prophets. But the time? Here's what He says: "But of that day and hour no one knows, neither the angels in heaven, nor the Son, but only the Father."

Unless Jesus was playing some kind of word games, He informed His disciples that He could not tell them when the end would come, simply because He did not know. Why this is a problem is immediately obvious. Jesus is supposed to be 100-percent God. God is omniscient—He knows everything. How, then, could there be something, even one thing, that Jesus by His own admission did not know?

Theologians have wrestled with this issue through the years. Most of the traditional explanations can be classified under three categories:

1. The total mystery theory. Those who hold this contend that we are here dealing with a matter for which there is no reasonable human explanation. God's ways are above our ways, and we do well to admit that we cannot understand this one.

2. The human Jesus theory. There are many liberal theologians who deny the deity of Christ. They never thought He really was God in the first place, and here is proof for their point. But in proving their point, they also have the much more difficult task of explaining away such passages as: "In the beginning was the Word, and the Word was with God, and the Word was God . . . . And the Word became flesh and dwelt among us" (John 1:1, 14). The human Jesus theory is unacceptable to evangelical Christians.

3. The two-channel theory. This theory states that since Jesus was both divine and human, He switched back and forth between the two natures constantly. At times He was God. At other times He was human. When He changed water into wine, He was God. When He got hungry, He was human.

This last theory is by far the most prevalent theory among evangelicals, just taken for granted by many. It is satisfactory to a point, because it faithfully preserves the idea of the deity of Christ. But at other points it is weak. For many years I held this theory, but then I tried to apply it to Mark 13:32. From this point of view we would have to understand that Jesus was really saying to His disciples, "*Humanly speaking* I do not know when the end of the age will come." The assumption is that if at that moment He had chosen to speak as God, He would have known the time and could have told them. This in itself sounds suspicious.

Furthermore, if Jesus were speaking from His human nature at that moment, how could He have said that the angels did not know when the end would come either? There is no human way to know that. So the two-channel theory would have Jesus switching channels right in the middle of a sentence. It no longer seemed like good theology to me.

INCARNATION THEOLOGY

To me, a much more reasonable theory for understanding the relationship of Jesus' two natures is what I like to call the incarnation theology. The basis for this is a careful reading of the well-known passage in Philippians chapter 2. It is so important that I am going to quote it here:

> Let this mind be in you which was also in Christ Jesus, who, being in the form of God, did not consider it robbery to be equal with God, but made Himself of no reputation, taking the form of a servant, and coming in the likeness of men. And being found in appearance as a man, He humbled Himself and became obedient to the point of death, even the death of the cross (vv. 5-8).

As a starter, this passage affirms clearly that Jesus was 100-percent God. As God he had all the divine attributes, among which was omniscience. He was "equal with God."

Part and parcel of Jesus' accepting an incarnation and taking on a human nature was agreeing to be obedient throughout His life on earth.

While Jesus was God, through the Incarnation He became unequal. It is obvious that after the Incarnation Jesus was different from before. How, then, did He become unequal? Clearly, it was not by giving up His divinity, because He was always 100-percent God. No, Jesus became unequal to the Father not by giving up anything, but by taking on something the Father did not have. He received a human nature, "taking the form of a servant, and coming in the likeness of men." From that time on, Jesus was different from both the Father and the Holy Spirit, because they have only one nature. Jesus had two.

Part and parcel of Jesus' accepting an incarnation and taking on a human nature was agreeing to be obedient throughout His life on earth. He "became obedient to the point of death, even the death of the cross."

Understanding Jesus in His incarnation as an obedient servant is crucial to understanding the dynamics of His ministry here on earth. What was the nature of His obedience? For one thing, it was voluntary. Nothing forced Jesus to do it. For another, it was temporary. It would end at His death. Furthermore, through this pact of obedience with the Father, Jesus agreed to suspend the use of His divine attributes for the duration of His earthly ministry. Notice, I am not suggesting He ever ceased to possess His divine attributes. But even though He had them, He voluntarily agreed not to use them.

If the above is correct, then we have a theological key: *The only nature that Jesus used while He was on earth was His human nature.*

I fully realize that this sounds strange to many evangelicals, because it is so different from the usual two-channel theory. I will never forget that during my ordination examination over 30 years ago, I happened to mention it without realizing it would shock some members of my committee. They did finally vote to ordain me, but it was a close call, and the ordination was contingent on my promise to do some more reading on the relationship of the two natures of Christ. I kept my promise, but the net result was that I kept my original ideas as well. Still, through the years I found the position to be a very lonely one.

More recently I was overjoyed when I found strong support for this idea from one of today's most respected systematic theologians, my colleague Colin Brown of Fuller Seminary. In his book *That You May Believe,* he dedicates his entire Part II to "What do the Miracle Stories Tell Us of Jesus?" He calls his point of view a "Spirit Christology." With skillful detail he rejects the two-channel theory "put together by traditional apologetics of Jesus the divine Son of God, doing the miracles in his own right, as it were." Brown says, "Jesus' miracles are given a prominent place, but they are not attributed to Jesus as the Second Person of the Trinity. They are not presented as manifestations of his personal divinity."[3] I highly recommend Brown's work for those who want more depth.

Jesus as the Second Adam

In order to help bring the picture into focus, let me elaborate on it by first exploring the meaning of Jesus as the second Adam, and then seeing what Jesus Himself had to say about it.

When Adam was in the Garden of Eden, he had the power to eat the forbidden fruit at any time. But he had entered into a pact of obedience with God that he would not use this power and eat the fruit. An important means of maintaining Adam's intimate relationship with God was his obedience. The parallel with Jesus is obvious. Jesus had the power to use His divine attributes at any time during His earthly ministry, but so long as He obeyed the Father, He could not use them.

The apostle Paul refers to Jesus as the last Adam. He says, "The first man was of the earth, made of dust" and then "the second Man [Adam] is the Lord from heaven" (1 Cor. 15:47). What does this imply?

One implication is that both Adam and Jesus were created, so to speak from scratch and not, as the rest of us are, from previous human beings. The details of Adam's creation are clearly revealed. We do not have the same details of Jesus' creation, however, except that we are told He had no earthly father.

We evangelicals are accustomed to accepting the fact that Jesus had no genetic relationship to Joseph. He was conceived, not by sperm, but by the Holy Spirit. Beyond that, although we do not often think of it, it might well be that He was also conceived without a human egg. If so, He had no genetic relationship to Mary either.

Mary could well have served essentially as a human

incubator, providing the uterus, placenta, the hormones and the nutrition for Jesus before birth, just as she supplied the milk for His nourishment after the birth. But could we accept the possibility that Jesus had no more genetic relationship to past human beings than did Adam? If so, it would help clarify why Jesus could be called the second Adam.

This might also give us a clue to another parallel between Jesus and Adam, namely, that neither one was contaminated with original sin. Theologians postulate that original sin is passed genetically from generation to generation. Although this is admittedly a minor point, if Jesus had no genetic relationship to either Mary or Joseph, it would help us understand how this could be. Jesus might have been referring to His nongenetic past by pointing out to the Pharisees that He could not be a son of David, since David called him Lord (see Matt. 22:41-46).

Of course, while it might be true that neither Jesus nor Adam had genetic ties with past humans, they nevertheless were not the same. Adam was created from the dust of the ground—he had only one nature, a human nature. Jesus came from heaven—He had a divine nature as well as a human nature (see 1 Cor. 15:47).

The Temptation

A much more important implication of Jesus' being the second Adam for the point I am making in this chapter is related to their temptations. I mentioned previously that both Adam and Jesus had entered into pacts of obedience with the Father. And when Satan tempted them, obedience was the jugular he went for in both cases. For Adam, it was the forbidden fruit. For Jesus, it was the use of His divine attributes.

I know that some disagree, but I happen to believe that Jesus' temptation was for real. In other words, Jesus could have sinned. If He couldn't, the whole thing would have been not much more than a charade, in my opinion. In what way could He have sinned? He could have broken His pact of obedience with the Father by using His divine attributes.

Satan apparently knew this very well, because all three of Jesus' temptations touched the very point of using His divine attributes. Jesus could have changed the stones to bread simply by using His divine omnipotence. He could have called angels to save Him if He had jumped from the Temple, since He was God and Commander-in-Chief of the angels. He could have taken over the kingdoms of the world if He chose to, even without worshiping Satan, since He was King of kings and Lord of lords. But He did none of the above, because any one of them would have broken the pact of obedience that Jesus had made with the Father as a part of His incarnation. When Jesus successfully resisted these temptations, the defeat of the enemy had begun in earnest.

This reminds me of something my friend Edward Murphy, vice president of Overseas Crusades, once told me. Murphy, who incidentally taught at Biola University for many years, has the gift of exorcism, and he has been greatly used of God in the ministry of deliverance from demonic oppression. His teaching on spiritual warfare is the best I have heard. On one occasion he was engaged in a particularly animated dialogue with an unusually intelligent evil spirit who did not want to leave a certain person. Ed said, "Do you realize that my Master has defeated your master?" The demon had to confess that it was true. Taunting the demon a little (he admits he probably should never have done this), Ed said, "Where did my Master defeat your master?" He expected him to answer that it was on Calvary. Instead, to Murphy's surprise, the demon said, "In the wilderness temp-

> *Since Jesus was experiencing life through His human nature, it should come as no surprise that He experienced life just as we do, except that He did not sin.*

tation." I don't believe that demons make particularly reliable theological statements, but this one, to say the least, is quite fascinating.

Satan tried one last time in the Garden of Gethsemane. He attacked the same point, this time in a moment of particular weakness. Jesus would have done almost anything to avoid being crucified; anything, that is, except break His pact of obedience with the Father. Again, He could have called legions of angels to wipe out the Roman legions. But if He had done so, the plan of salvation would have been over, the kingdom of God would have retreated, and Satan would still be in charge.

The Source of Jesus' Power

We need not attempt to explain away statements such as Hebrews 4:15 that Jesus was "in all points tempted as we are, yet without sin." Since Jesus was experiencing life through His human nature, it should come as no surprise that He experienced life just as we do, except that He did not sin. Better than we, He knew how to obey the Father.

But this also leads us to understand more clearly how Jesus performed miracles, healed the sick and cast out demons. Negatively, we know for sure that it was not done through His divine attributes. Positively, we see that all of Jesus' supernatural ministry was done, not by Himself, but by the power of the Holy Spirit. Not that He couldn't have done miracles Himself. After all, He was God. But, because of His voluntary obedience, He refused to do them, even when challenged directly by His chief adversary.

The apostle Peter knew this, and he explained it when he preached in the house of Cornelius. He told how Jesus "went about doing good and healing all who were oppressed by the devil." But did He do it on His own? No, He did it only because "God anointed him with the Holy Spirit and with power" (see Acts 10:38). Anointing implies that something is imparted to Him outside Himself. But if He were operating through His divine attributes, He could receive nothing outside Himself, because God is all in all.

What did Jesus have to say about this? A great deal. As a starter, He said, "The Son can do nothing of Himself, but what He sees the Father do" (John 5:19). Jesus depended on the Father at all times.

Did you ever think what Jesus was like when He was growing up? He probably cried when He was hungry, just like all the babies we know. And He needed potty training. I sing it, but I don't believe the Christmas carol that says, "The little Lord Jesus no crying he makes." He had to learn to talk Aramaic by trial and error. He couldn't understand a word of Chinese or Aztec, because He never learned those languages. I imagine His parents scolded Him from time to time. He probably made His share of apprentice mistakes in the carpenter shop and needed to be corrected by Joseph. He got indigestion when He ate bad food or stuffed Himself too much on a holiday. In fact, the people in His hometown of Nazareth thought He was such a normal Jewish boy that the suggestion that Jesus was Messiah made no sense to them.

But while He may have been like other boys His age, He was also unlike them in that He was totally obedient to the Father. The first incident out of the ordinary that we know about was when He stayed behind in Jerusalem to dialogue with the Jewish teachers. Remember what He said to His parents by way of explanation? "Did you not know that I must be about My Father's business?" (Luke 2:49). Mary and Joseph didn't seem to understand. But we do, because we have John 5:19, which explains that the Son does only "what He sees the Father do."

We might think that Jesus' obedience was automatic. That would be true if He were using His divine attributes, but He wasn't. Because He was operating as a 100-percent human being, He had to learn obedience, which is exactly what Hebrews 5:8 says: "Though He was a Son, yet He learned obedience by the things which He suffered." Presumably, as the years went by, He became better and better at obeying the Father.

When Jesus cast out demons, it was not by His own power. He said, "I cast out demons with the finger of God" (Luke 11:20). When he passed judgment, it was with authority delegated to Him by the Father. He said, "For the Father judges no one, but has committed all judgment to the Son" (John 5:22). And then, "I can of Myself do nothing. As I hear, I judge" (v. 30). Where did

Jesus' teaching come from? "Whatever I speak, just as the Father has told Me, so I speak" (12:50). No one had power to take Jesus' life without His personal agreement. He said, "I have power to lay it down, and I have power to take it again." Did He refer to His inherent divine power? No, for He explained, "This command I have received from my Father" (10:18).

In all this, Jesus did do something that no other human being can legitimately do: He accepted the worship of others. He could do that because, through it all, He never stopped being 100-percent God. The wise men came to worship Him (see Matt. 2:2). A blind man Jesus healed worshiped Him (see John 9:38). A demonized man worshiped Him even before the demons were cast out (see Mark 5:6). Because He always had a divine nature, Jesus did not have to respond as did Peter when Cornelius fell down and worshiped him: "Stand up; I myself am also a man" (Acts 10:26). Unlike Jesus, Peter had only one nature, a human nature.

The End of the Obedience

Jesus' pact of obedience was not forever. As we saw in Philippians 2:8, He "became obedient to the point of death, even the death of the cross." Many who do not understand that Jesus was operating from His human nature have a hard time with His agonizing statement from the cross: "My God, my God, why have You forsaken Me?" (Matt. 27:46). But it makes good sense if we suppose that at this particular point the Father chose not to reveal to Jesus exactly why this was happening, and Jesus' question was a normal human reaction.

When Jesus said, "Into Your hands I commend My spirit" (Luke 23:46), the pact of obedience was all over.

He once again began using His divine attributes.

One clue we find for understanding that a change took place at that time came after Jesus' resurrection when He was giving the final teaching to His disciples. They asked him, "Lord, will You at this time restore the kingdom to Israel?" (Acts 1:6). The question was similar to the one which raised the problem of Mark 13:32. At that time, before His death, Jesus did not know the answer, and He said so. But this time, after His death, He did know because He was using His divine attributes. Therefore, He said, "It is not for you to know times or seasons which the Father has put in His own authority" (Acts 1:7).

DOING THE WORKS OF THE FATHER

Once we understand that Jesus, during His earthly ministry, did not do His own works, but rather the works of the Father, tremendous possibilities of ministry are opened up for us. As I mentioned at the beginning of the chapter, Jesus promised His followers that they would do the same works He did and even greater ones were not beyond possibility. This promise is for us as well, because "Jesus Christ is the same yesterday, today, and forever" (Heb. 13:8). We receive power to do the works of the Father through the Holy Spirit.

What happened to Jesus can happen to us. In the last chapter I mentioned how Jesus announced His agenda in the synagogue of Nazareth at the beginning of His ministry by listing some of the signs of the kingdom. He prefaced those remarks, however, by a very significant statement of His relationship to the Holy Spirit. He mentioned three things: (1) The Holy Spirit "is upon

Me"—Jesus was filled with the Spirit; (2) The Holy Spirit "has anointed Me"—Jesus was empowered by the Spirit; (3) The Holy Spirit "has sent Me"— Jesus was commissioned by the Spirit (see Luke 4:18). By the same Holy Spirit we can be filled, empowered and commissioned to do the works of the Father.

It seems that whenever the suggestion of doing the same works that Jesus did is raised, the more skeptical souls will argue against it by pointing out that no one they know, in the Pentecostal and charismatic movements or out of them, heals the sick, casts out demons or performs miracles as well and as frequently as Jesus did. This is true, and it is also understandable. While we have access to the same power that Jesus did, we are not Jesus. He had two advantages that we do not have; namely, He had no original sin and He had no actual sin. As a result, He enjoyed three benefits that no one else has:

1. Jesus had a completely open and unrestricted channel to the Father. He never found an obstruction to His prayer, and therefore He always knew perfectly what the Father was doing.

2. Jesus had total faith in the power of the Holy Spirit to do through Him the works of the Father. He said that God did not give Him the Holy Spirit by measure (see John 3:34). His filling of the Holy Spirit was complete at all times.

3. Jesus never wavered from total obedience to the Father. He could have slipped, but He never did.

While these qualities set Jesus apart from any other human, they also give us clues as to how we can see greater power in our own ministries. We need to develop our own prayer lives by praying longer and with more intensity and with fasting. We need to improve the quality of our faith by being open to the filling of the Holy Spirit. And we need to obey God more consistently. This involves living holy and godly lives according to biblical standards, and learning to be more perceptive in seeing what the Father is doing. If we succeed, our prayers will be better heard, for "If we ask anything according to His will, He hears us." (1 John 5:14)

No one will match Jesus in the effectiveness of His works of the miraculous any more than matching His love. But while Christian growth and maturity do not mean that we shall be perfect, they do mean that we can and should be closer to that in the future than we are today. We can love better and we can heal better.

In a dialogue I was having with a friend who did not believe that the gift of healing was for today, I brought up the fact that I thought I had the gift. This disturbed him, so he said, "Well, if you have the gift of healing, why don't you go down and empty the Huntington Hospital?" My response was that I would if that's what I saw the Father doing. But otherwise it would be stupid, because when I heal I am not doing my works, but the Father's.

I believe that Jesus operated on the same principle. The nearest thing to a hospital that we read about in the Gospels is the pool of Bethesda. When Jesus went there, He did not heal all those who had gathered around the pool, but only one. Why only one? How did He know which one to pick? Evidently because that was all the Father wanted to do at the time, and Jesus did only what He saw the Father do.

HOW JESUS PASSED THE POWER

None of the Gospel writers take more care than John in

explaining how the power of Jesus in inaugurating the kingdom of God was passed on to those who would be the agents of the extension of the kingdom after His death. Almost one-fourth of his Gospel (chap. 13-17) deals with Jesus' extended teaching on the subject. It is for this reason that such a large number of Scripture texts quoted in this chapter have come from John. Let me summarize my ideas on passing the power by tracing Jesus' train of thought through this crucial passage.

In chapter 13 Jesus prepares His disciples for the trauma of the transition. His main concern is that His disciples would understand as thoroughly as possible what type of ministry they would have after the Crucifixion. They had been with Him for three years and it would not be easy for them to continue on their own without His physical presence. He washes their feet and explains to them why, as leaders, they need first to be servants. He breaks the disturbing news that He is going away, and says, "Where I am going, you cannot come" (John 13:33).

In chapter 14 (these chapter divisions are approximate, not precise) Jesus teaches His disciples that the source of the power for their future ministry would be the Father. He explains to them that their relationship to Him carried with it a relationship to the Father. He says, "If you had known Me, you would have known my Father also; and from now on you know Him and have seen Him" (14:7). Jesus' leaving will not disturb this relationship to the Father, and they can look forward to being in His Father's house with many mansions. He tells them that because Jesus' own authority and power came from the Father, theirs will also and therefore they will be able to do the same works and even greater ones.

In chapter 15 we find that Jesus is the director of the

power. He is the vine and if the disciples abide in Him they will bear much fruit. He stresses the need for them to keep His commandments, reminding them that they did not choose Him, but He chose them. And then He warns them that, just as Jesus suffered, so must they expect to suffer as they serve Him because the servant is not above the master.

In chapter 16, Jesus teaches them that the channel of the power that comes from the Father is the Holy Spirit. So, Jesus tells them, "It is to your advantage that I go away" (v. 7), because only then will the Holy Spirit come. He will be a helper, He will convict the world of sin, righteousness and judgment, He will guide them into all truth and He will glorify Jesus. He acts on the authority of the Son: "He will take of what is Mine and declare it to you" (v. 14).

Finally, in chapter 17, Jesus concludes with prayer. He prays for Himself, He prays for His disciples and He prays for all believers.

The power that Jesus passed to His disciples did not arrive until the day of Pentecost. But when it did, it came to stay, and it provides the basis for the ministry that the third wave advocates: doing the works of the Father through the power brought by the Holy Spirit, just as Jesus did them.

Notes

1. Ray Stedman, *Acts 1-12: Birth of the Body* (Ventura, CA: Regal Books, Div. of Gospel Light Publications, 1974), p. 106.
2. Michael Harper, *The Healings of Jesus* (Downers Grove, IL: 1986), p. 124.
3. Colin Brown, *That You May Believe: Miracles and Faith Then and Now* (Grand Rapids, MI: Wm. B. Eerdmans Pub. Co., 1985), p. 97. Another supporter of this viewpoint is Thomas A. Smail in *Reflected Glory: The Spirit in Christ and in Christmas* (London: Hodder and Stoughton, 1975). On page 70 he says: "There has been a tendency in Protestant circles, not with-

out its origin in Calvin, to distribute the attributes of Christ between his divinity and humanity, so that his power to work signs and miracles is seen as the power of his unique divinity. The consequence is obvious; if his miracles had nothing to do with his humanity, if divine power was not communicated to his human nature as a charismatic gift, then obviously that power has nothing to do with our humanity either . . . . With this kind of Christology all kinds of dispensationalising of the gifts of the Holy Spirit are very much at home."

SIX

TUNING IN TO THE POWER

Jesus came to bring the kingdom of God to earth. He called His disciples, trained them and promised that they would have access to the same power that worked through Him during His ministry. And just before He left them for good, He said, "But tarry in the city of Jerusalem until you are endued with power from on high" (Luke 24:49).

THE GREAT COMMISSION

The disciples' task, for which they were to receive the power of the Holy Spirit, was to carry the blessings of the kingdom throughout all the earth. This was Jesus'

Great Commission. The reason for the power was clear: "But you shall receive power when the Holy Spirit has come upon you; and you shall be witnesses to Me in Jerusalem, and in all Judea and Samaria, and to the end of the earth" (Acts 1:8). Power from God is to be focused on world evangelization.

In Mark 16 the Great Commission and power also go together. Jesus commands His disciples to "Go into all the world and preach the gospel to every creature" (Mark 16:15). Then He mentions the signs that will accompany those who believe: casting out demons, speaking with new tongues, taking up serpents, drinking poison with no harm, and healing the sick.

Likewise in Matthew Jesus says, "Go therefore and make disciples of all the nations" (28:19). He tells them they can do it because "all authority has been given to Me" (v. 18) and "lo, I am with you always" (v. 20). Authority for what? The Greek word used here is *exousia*, the same word translated "power" in Matthew 10:1: "He gave them power over unclean spirits, to cast them out, and to heal all kinds of sickness and all kinds of disease."

Part of the Great Commission involves "teaching them to observe all things that I have commanded you" (28:20). The disciples never forgot the first time Jesus sent them out on their own. Their message was a message of both word and deed. They were to "preach, saying, 'The kingdom of heaven is at hand,'" and they were also to "heal the sick, cleanse the lepers, raise the dead, cast out demons" (10:7,8). If they were given power and commanded to heal the sick and cast out demons, that ministry was to be included in what they would teach others, and they did teach others to do it. Jesus passed the power to His disciples and they passed it to others.

POWER EVANGELISM IN THE ACTS AND EPISTLES

What evidence do we have that Jesus' power was truly passed on to His followers? The Book of Acts tells the story of the next 30 years, and virtually every chapter, with the exception of the long account of Paul's arrest and imprisonment, describes the signs and wonders that accompanied first-century evangelism.

When the power first comes in Acts 2, the gospel is communicated in Jerusalem through the vernacular languages of all those who had gathered for the feast of Pentecost. "Many wonders and signs were done through the apostles" (v. 43), and "the Lord added to the church daily those who were being saved" (v. 47). Then Peter and John heal the lame man at the Temple gate (see Acts 3). Soon the number of male believers is 5,000. Peter and John pray that they may speak God's Word with all boldness and "that signs and wonders may be done through the name of Your holy Servant Jesus" (4:30).

The apostles witness to Jesus "with great power" (v. 33). How awesome is this power? Awesome enough to kill Ananias and Sapphira when they lied to God and to bring great fear of offending God upon the church (see 5:11). Still, "believers were increasingly added to the Lord" because "through the hands of the apostles many signs and wonders were done among the people" (5:12-14).

Then comes Stephen, who, "full of faith and power, did great wonders and signs among the people" (6:8). And under Philip's ministry "the multitudes with one accord heeded the things spoken by Philip, hearing and seeing the miracles which he did" (8:6). So, while up to now we see the power channeled largely through the apostles, the circle widens to include at least two of the seven Hellenistic leaders ordained in Acts 6. If Stephen and Philip were using power evangelism, it is reasonable to assume that the other five of their group were doing so as well, even though we don't have the details.

The drama seems to heighten as Peter heals Aeneas, who was paralyzed for eight years (see 9:33,34), and then raises Dorcas from the dead (vv. 36-41). He tells Cornelius that Jesus "went about doing good and healing all who were oppressed by the devil, for God was with Him" (10:38). Later Peter is dramatically released from prison by an angel (see 12:7).

Saul, the persecutor of the Church, becomes the apostle Paul through a dramatic display of God's power on the road to Damascus (see 9:1-19). Through Paul Elymas the sorcerer is made blind and a government official is saved (see 13:6-12). In Iconium Paul and Barnabas speak boldly, and God grants "signs and wonders to be done by their hands" (14:3). In Lystra they pray for a crippled man "And he leaped and walked" (v. 10). Paul casts a demon out of a slave girl in Philippi (see 16:18), a supernatural earthquake springs him and his friends from prison (see v. 26), and when handkerchiefs that had touched Paul's body were brought to the sick, "the diseases left them and the evil spirits went out of them" (19:11,12). Many other illustrations of power evangelism are associated with Paul's ministry.

It is natural, then, that Paul would talk about power evangelism in the letters he writes to the churches he planted. He reminds the Thessalonians that "our gospel did not come to you in word only, but also in power, and in the Holy Spirit" (1 Thess. 1:5). He mentions to the Galatians that God "supplies the Spirit to you and works miracles among you" (Gal. 3:5). He warns the Ephesians that "we do not wrestle against flesh and blood, but against principalities, against powers" (Eph. 6:12). In the letter to the Philippians he shares his joy that his friend Epaphroditus was healed by God from a sickness that almost took his life (see 2:27). He declares to the Corinthians that "the kingdom of God is not in word but in power" (1 Cor. 4:20), and that his ministry among them was "in demonstration of the Spirit and of power" (2:4). He tells the Corinthians about the spiritual gifts of healing and miracles and prophecy and discernment of spirits among others (see 1 Cor. 12), and reminds them of the many miracles and wonders he performed among them (see 2 Cor. 12:12).

Paul did not plant the church at Rome, but when he writes to the believers there in preparation for a visit toward the end of his ministry, he sums up his evangelistic work by saying that he has always spoken of the things that Christ has done through him among the Gentiles "in mighty signs and wonders, by the power of the Spirit of God" (Rom. 15:18,19). This sounds like power evangelism par excellence.

Other Epistles pick up the theme. The writer to the Hebrews says that the word of salvation came with "God also bearing witness both with signs and wonders, with various miracles, and gifts of the Holy Spirit" (Heb. 2:4). And James, known for his impatience with faith without works, gives instructions to anyone who is sick. They are to call the elders for anointing with oil and prayer, "and the prayer of faith will save the sick" (Jas. 5:15).

GOD'S POWER THROUGH HISTORY

The New Testament records continuous power evangelism. But what happened afterwards?

Toward the beginning of the century Princeton theologian Benjamin B. Warfield established a theological mind-set for three generations of evangelical Christians through his book *Miracles: Yesterday and Today, Real and Counterfeit.* He concludes that "the power of working miracles was not extended beyond the disciples upon whom the Apostles conferred it by imposition of their hands." As he interprets the records, he sees a gradual diminishing of signs and wonders until they "ceased entirely at the death of the last individual on whom the hands of the Apostles had been laid."[1]

Warfield's book was written in 1918 when Pentecostals were still considered by many evangelicals as a false cult along with Christian Scientists and Mormons. So his point of view, which furnished instant ammunition, rapidly became fashionable and many still hold it. But since his book was first published in 1918, much more historical research has been done, particularly by a new breed of Pentecostal scholars, but also by others.

What this research is showing is that the power Jesus passed to His disciples for healing the sick and casting out demons did, in fact, continue through the ages. There seem to have been historical periods in which miraculous ministries were more prominent than in others, but some of this at least might be attributed to our lack of knowledge. Digging into the past and uncovering new facts is what keeps historians in business. The more research done, the more evidence we have that Warfield is mistaken.

In his influential book *Evangelism in the Early Church*, Michael Green of Regent College finds that from the beginning Christians "went out into the world as exorcizers and healers as well as preachers." And this "continued throughout not only the apostolic church but into the second and third centuries, to look no further."[2]

Not all scholars see this. Consider, for example, an interesting contrast between two contemporary analyses of the spread of the gospel among the Gentiles in the early days. Derek Tidball, writing purely from a sociological viewpoint, sees the dominant concerns of the Gentiles as moral and sexual ethics, family relationships, relationships at work and attitudes to the state. He attributes the success of the spread of the gospel among the Gentiles to the exclusiveness of Christianity, the openness to all classes and races, the promises of happiness in another world and benefits in the here and now, chiefly those of belonging to the Christian family.[3] Notable is his lack of reference to their fear of evil spirits and their desire for physical healing, and the power that accompanied Christian preaching to deal with these needs.

The contrast comes with Ramsay MacMullen, to whom I have referred previously. Even from the perspective of a secular historian, he comes to the conclusion that what we are here calling power evangelism was the "chief instrument of conversion" among pagan Gentiles.[4] So far as religious loyalty was concerned, for both Christian and non-Christian in the Gentile world of the first few centuries, "the essential and, so far as we can tell, the only thing believed in was some supernatural power to bestow benefits."[5]

THE CONVERSION OF EUROPE

But this does not stop with the first few centuries. Charles Henry Robinson, who chronicles the history of the conversion of Europe, is somewhat of a skeptic when it comes to accounts of the miraculous. He says that "when we consider the unscientific character of the age in which these miracles were recorded and the impossibility of obtaining evidence that can satisfy the critical historian, we cannot assume the occurrence of a miracle in any single case." Nevertheless, supernatural signs and wonders are so prominent in the histories of missionary work among the peoples of Europe that "we cannot afford to neglect these stories altogether."[6]

Assuming, then, that he neglects as many as possible, Robinson recounts incident after incident of power evangelism. Patrick of Ireland works many miracles; Germanus of Auxerre stills a storm on the English Channel; as he evangelizes France, Martin of Tours not only cuts down a sacred spirit tree but stands right where it is expected to fall and is unharmed; Columbanus controls wild beasts through divine power; in Southern Italy both Benedict and Barbatus evangelize by challenging Satan head on and destroying sacred groves; in Holland Wulfram raises a boy from the dead; Boniface dares to topple the sacred Thunderer's Oak in Germany; Bernard prevents fire from burning him; in Norway King Olaf, on the challenge of a pagan leader, sees God answer specific prayer concerning the weather.

By the time of the Reformation so many spurious claims for the miraculous had been mixed with the authentic ones in the Roman Catholic Church that the Reformers tended to distance themselves from signs and wonders. However, many Reformers did not totally reject ministries of the supernatural, particularly during crises in their own ministries. The story is told, for example, of Martin Luther's anguish with the medical prognosis that his associate, Phillip Melanchthon, had a sickness that would take his life. Luther knelt, prayed for his recovery, and the condition was reversed instantly.[7] John Wesley is said to have healed his lame horse through prayer.[8] John Knox' son-in-law, John Welsh, reportedly knelt and prayed for 36 hours over the corpse of a young count who was one of his strong supporters, begging God to give the man back to him, and God answered his prayer.[9]

Several of today's non-Pentecostal denominations are more rooted in powerful ministries of the miraculous than many current members realize, because, either intentionally or unintentionally, that particular dimension of their history has not been emphasized. For example, in 1885 General William Booth, founder of the Salvation Army, reported the "recent remarkable signs and wonders wrought amongst us" and wrote his comrades about the extraordinary gifts of the Spirit such as tongues, healings and miracles. He said that he knew of nothing in the Bible or in experience "to show they would not be as useful today as in any previous period of the Church's history."[10]

Part of the revival in the Swedish Lutheran Church, which gave birth to the Evangelical Covenant Church, was the appearance of "Criers," young people supernaturally anointed by the Holy Spirit for preaching and prophecy.[11] A. B. Simpson, founder of the Christian and Missionary Alliance, gave a high priority to divine healing in the late 1800s, and many Alliance Churches had a powerful healing ministry. The Church of the Nazarene stressed healing in its early years, as did the Quakers, the Mennonites, the Moravians and many others.

Several authors of recent books on healing ministries have included valuable historical data, tracing signs and wonders through history. We are indebted to writers such as Morton T. Kelsey,[12] J. Sidlow Baxter,[13] John Wimber,[14] Rex Gardner,[15] John Gunstone[16] and others who remind us that Jesus is the same yesterday, today and forever and that the power He passed to the disciples has been passed on to us today.

WORLDVIEW: BELIEVING IS SEEING

If you are an evangelical, you probably believe that Peter raised Dorcas from the dead. But do you believe that Wulfram of Holland or John Welsh of Scotland raised the dead? How about Columbanus controlling wild beasts or Germanus stilling a storm or John Wesley healing a horse?

More than we sometimes know or like to admit, our answers to such questions as these depend heavily on our particular worldview. This helps explain how one scholar can look at a period of history and not see signs and wonders as significant, while another, equally as sincere and intelligent, can look at the same period and see them as a major dimension of Christian life and witness. The two are working out of different worldviews in general or different paradigms in particular. But worldview not only influences how we see history, it permeates every part of our daily lives.

Lewis Smedes, for example, points out how worldview determines our attitudes toward something as important as ethical issues. "We disagree," he says, "because we do not *see* the same things." Or else, "we do *not* see the same significance in the things we are both looking at."[17]

What, exactly, is meant by worldview? My colleague, Charles H. Kraft, widely regarded as a top expert in the field, defines worldview as "The culturally patterned basic understandings (e.g., assumptions, presuppositions, beliefs, etc.) of REALITY by which the members of a society organize and live their lives."[18] The word REALITY is capitalized because Kraft means the objective world out there as God only sees it. Our point of view is always

> *If people believe that God does not heal today, they will not be able to see divine healing, no matter what quantity of documentation or proof is provided.*

a small letter *reality* because none of us sees REALITY as God sees it. Nevertheless our perceptions of reality are valid and useful for living out our human lives. But we must never forget that other peoples both near to us and far from us have different understandings of reality, or different worldviews. In other words, as Smedes says, it is possible for individuals to see the same thing differently.

I love the story Colin Brown tells about the King of Siam. It seems that back in the seventeenth century the King of Siam was having a very pleasant talk with the Dutch ambassador. He was enthralled by the stories of life in far-off Holland. Enthralled, that is, until the ambassador began telling the king, who had lived his entire life in the tropics, about the winter in Holland and how water would get so hard an elephant could walk on it. The king replied, "Hitherto I have believed the strange things you have told me, because I look upon you as a sober fair man; but now I am sure you lie."[19] The king's worldview, or as Brown calls it "frame of reference," could not process the information the ambassador brought him. In that particular case the ambassador's reality happened to be closer to REALITY than the king's. In other cases the king's might have been closer.

Worldview is extremely important when it comes to assessing the need for or the value of a healing ministry. If people believe that God does not heal today, they will not be able to see divine healing, no matter what quantity of documentation or proof is provided. Convincing a skeptic is a thankless effort. Jesus Himself would not perform a miracle to convince skeptics because He knew it wouldn't do any good. Because they did not believe, they would not be able to see what Jesus did. In a true sense, believing is seeing.

Rex Gardner, from the point of view of a physician who also believes in divine healing, wrestles with this issue. He gives a case study of a patient with Waterhouse-Friderichsen syndrome, which had caused pneumonia and permanent blindness. When healing prayer was offered, she recovered. But the physicians attending this patient could not see that the healings were the work of God. Gardner comments concerning the woman whose sight was restored, "Despite the fact that the four consultants who saw her on admission remain confident as to their diagnosis, its accuracy is called in doubt by those unable to explain her survival."[20] What's their problem? Obviously it is the same as the King of Siam's—worldview. They can only see if they believe.

THE EXCLUDED MIDDLE

The issue of worldview is extremely significant in cross-cultural ministries. I recall a fascinating theological

examination in which the faculty of an American theological seminary was interviewing a prospective faculty
member. The difference between this exam and others
was that the candidate happened to be Chinese. When

*Very few statements of faith . . . deal with
the working of the supernatural in daily
experience. They frequently mention the
work of the Holy Spirit in saving souls, but
not in healing bodies.*

asked, "What is your general impression of the seminary's statement of faith?" he answered, "I think it is fine
and can agree with it as far as it goes. I must say, however, that it would not be adequate for an Asian institution."

Predictably, his response provoked a lengthy discussion. He mentioned that the statement of faith had no
section on supernatural forces of good and evil, such as
angels and demons. It had mentioned Satan in passing,
but contained no explicit reference to his personality or
work in the world today. To the Asian believer, it failed to
reflect an important area of biblical revelation.

Not that the seminary in question was any different
from other American Christian institutions. Very few
statements of faith of American churches of denominations or parachurch organizations deal with the working
of the supernatural in daily experience. They frequently
mention the work of the Holy Spirit in saving souls, but
not in healing bodies. They mention power for living a
godly life, but not for casting out demons.

Why is this?

It gets us back to worldview. Our traditional Anglo-

American worldview is increasingly materialistic and naturalistic. As I have mentioned previously, secular humanism has penetrated our Christian institutions to a surprising degree. Even though a large majority of Americans believe there is a God, His contact with our daily lives is seen as minimal. Our worldview is heavily influenced by secular science. We are taught from childhood to suppose that almost everything that happens in daily life has causes and effects, which are governed by scientific laws.

This is not so in the Third World. Most people there live with the reality of demons and evil spirits as a part of daily life. Their worldview tells them that shamans, witches, witch doctors and mediums have the power to control the supernatural forces that cause disease, poverty, oppression, crop failure, hurricanes, barrenness, drought and mental illness. When Christianity is presented to them as an option, their uppermost question is whether the God of Christianity has enough power to solve life's problems. In light of the New Testament, there is a strong possibility that their worldview might be nearer to REALITY at this point than ours.

My colleague Paul G. Hiebert calls this phenomenon "the flaw of the excluded middle." He mentions that when John the Baptist sent his messengers to ask Jesus if He was the Messiah, the answer came back in terms of power to heal the sick and cast out demons rather than in terms of logical proofs. "When I read that passage as a missionary in India," Hiebert says, "I had a sense of uneasiness." He confesses that he was trained to present Christ with rational arguments rather than through demonstrations of supernatural power. He adds, "In particular, the confrontation with spirits that appeared so natural a part of Christ's ministry belonged in my mind to a separate world of the miraculous—far from ordinary everyday experience."[21]

Hiebert goes on to point out that the worldview of most non-Westerners is three-tiered. The top tier is high religion based on cosmic personalities or forces. The bottom tier is everyday life: marriage, raising children, planting crops, sickness and health, material prosperity and what have you. The middle zone includes the normal way these everyday phenomena are influenced by superhuman and supernatural forces.

Our Western worldview is different. We are able to handle a top tier of cosmic religion and are most comfortable if all supernatural activity is relegated there. Our bottom tier is governed by scientific laws. We see little need for a middle zone where these areas of life are in constant contact with each other. In fact, if any one begins to take the middle zone too seriously and talks about the daily influence of supernatural powers both of good and of evil, we tend to think they are a bit superstitious and we try to persuade them to be more scientific.

This Western mind-set was clearly illustrated in a recent article in *Christianity Today*, "A Surgeon's View of Divine Healing." In it the surgeon says that he and faith healers both want to help people, but they have vastly different styles. He says, "I believe in the divine component of healing. But my own contributions to patients come after years of study and the application of rigid scientific principles to laws governing human physiology." He is disturbed that some Christians today "seem to promise an entirely new kind of medicine, an instantaneous healing that defies the normal process of science."[22] Hiebert would say he is typical of many Westerners in exhibiting an excluded middle.

In missionary work, the net result of the excluded

middle is that Western missionaries are often perceived as being agents of secularization. Our scientific approach seems to many of them to remove God from important areas of life, such as agriculture, medicine, reproduction and social relationships. Hiebert comments that "this approach confines God's work in people's lives purely to matters of ultimate salvation." Of course, ultimate salvation is important, but so is "faith in the power of prayer and in God's concern with all areas of human life." Hiebert agrees that this worldview is difficult to reconcile "with that of the Bible, in which the supernatural dimensions of this world are clearly evident."[23]

THE POWER ENCOUNTER

When we talk about Western and non-Western worldviews, it is easy to suppose that no one in the U.S. has a non-Western worldview. This has never been true, but it is even less so today. American Indians, for example, have always been a part of our nation, and their worldview is much different from that of the typical Anglo-American. While a major portion of immigration in the past has been from European nations with similar worldviews, this is no longer the case. Large numbers of newly arriving Chinese, East Indians, Mexicans, Arabs, Filipinos, Jamaicans, Samoans, Koreans, Nigerians and many others are bringing with them different worldviews. Even among many traditional Anglo-Americans the excluded middle is disappearing.

Time magazine (Dec. 7, 1987) recently ran a cover story on the New Age Movement, which is rooted in a non-Western worldview. The growth of spiritism and witchcraft and Satan worship and the occult and horoscopes and Eastern religions is a significant new fact of our day right here at home.

In Europe, where a whole generation was born into a world that threatens itself with nuclear destruction, faith in science as the answer to human problems is weakening. A Baptist pastor from Romania said, "Belief in Communism is not our problem. No one believes in Communism anymore. Our problem is witchcraft, Eastern religions and mysticism, and the occult." From Germany a Campus Crusade worker reports young people turning in droves to the New Age Movement, astrology, parapsychology and the occult. Jack MacDonald of TEAM reports that "those who heal by witchcraft in France outnumber medical doctors, and there is one spirit medium for every 120 Frenchmen."[24] These new developments in history make power evangelism highly appropriate in traditionally Western nations as well as in the Third World.

For people in close touch with the spirit world, a style of evangelism that involves a power encounter is usually more effective than other ways of focusing the gospel message. While for some the issues of morality and guilt are at the top of the agenda, for many others the issues of fear and power are supreme. To missiologist Alan Tippett, one of the early exponents of power encounter evangelism, the power encounter can make all the difference as to whether an individual or a family or even a whole tribe receives or rejects the gospel. For many, Tippett says, the power encounter is seen as "an encounter between their old and their new God." To be involved in such an encounter takes a great deal of courage, for "they have rejected the supernatural resources on which they once relied, and are challenging the old power to harm them."[25]

The kind of power encounter I am speaking of is a visible, practical demonstration that Jesus Christ is more powerful than the spirits, powers or false gods worshiped or feared by the members of a given people group. While every conversion is a power encounter in a sense, since an individual is delivered from the power of darkness to the power of light (see Col. 1:13), I refer here to the more public visible challenge that pits God against Satan.

Timothy Warner of Trinity Evangelical Divinity School gives a good example of what I mean. He tells of some people in a small Muslim fishing village in the Philippines who directly challenged a Christian layperson to a power encounter. They said, "If you can cast the devil from the woman, we will truly believe and embrace immediately the faith in Jesus Christ." They set a time, the demon was cast out, the woman was healed and the whole village became Christian.[26]

Edward Murphy, whom I have mentioned previously, travels the world a great deal in his ministry with Overseas Crusades. In India he occasionally works with an evangelist named Patro, a strong proponent of the power encounter. In fact, according to Murphy, Patro and his team will enter a hostile Hindu village, call out the village priest and say loudly, "The God of Jesus Christ is the only true and living God—a God of power. Bring us the sickest person in your village." When they do, Patro prays for healing in public, and when the person is healed, hearts are quickly opened to the gospel. Sometimes demonized people are brought out, tied up or locked in a cage, and they are delivered.

The basic question that many people in the world, and here in the U.S., have today is: Does your God have more power than ours? Timothy Warner asks the disturbing question: "Are we willing to go head-to-head in a power encounter with spiritual practitioners who have a demonstrated track record of producing results?"[27] Since this ministry clearly involves warfare, it is easy to see why many Christians will steer clear of it. Warner confesses that he did for many years, but no longer. He says that if we avoid the power encounter, "we live below our privileges in the gospel, we forfeit a ministry to persons who desperately need the power available to them through the victory of Christ, and we give Satan the satisfaction of seeing God deprived of the glory which is rightfully His."[28]

A student of mine, Lisa Tunstall, is planting a new church in Inglewood, California with her husband John. She arrived late to class one day because at 1:30 that morning John had received an emergency phone call from a woman in his church. The woman was in a panic, and he heard strange voices in the background. When he arrived at her house, the woman was slouched in a chair staring at him, and a masculine voice came from her mouth, "You are the man of God? I have been waiting for you. Show me your power!"

John Tunstall is a minister of the Disciples of Christ, a denomination that does not stress power evangelism. But he and Lisa have been part of the third wave, so he knew he was in a power encounter. He snapped back at the spirit, "Show me your power!" Instantly a flower pot on a shelf exploded into pieces with a loud noise.

But John was ready for it. He said, "My power is the blood of the Lord Jesus Christ. In Jesus' name I command you to leave that woman." The evil spirit struggled. The woman slithered onto the floor like a snake, then writhed around. But the power of Jesus prevailed, the demon left, and the woman was completely well. Little wonder that the Tunstalls' congregation is approaching 500. They know what it is to be tuned into the power.

Notes _____

1. Benjamin B. Warfield, *Miracles: Yesterday and Today, Real and Counterfeit* (Grand Rapids, MI: Wm. B. Eerdmans Pub. Co., 1954), pp. 23,24. The first edition was published in 1918.
2. Michael Green, *Evangelism in the Early Church* (Grand Rapids, MI: Wm. B. Eerdmans Pub. Co., 1970), p. 189.
3. Derek Tidball, *The Social Context of the New Testament* (Grand Rapids, MI: Zondervan Publishing House, 1984), pp. 74-75.
4. Ramsay MacMullen, *Christianizing the Roman Empire* (New Haven, CT: Yale University Press, 1984), p. 27.
5. Ibid., p. 4.
6. Charles Henry Robinson, *The Conversion of Europe*, (London: Longmans, Green and Co., 1917), pp. 38,39.
7. See Willem J. Kooiman, *By Faith Alone: The Life of Martin Luther* (London: Lutterworth Press, 1954), p. 192.
8. See Morton T. Kelsey, *Healing and Christianity* (New York: Harper and Row, 1973), p. 235.
9. See Rex Gardner, *Healing Miracles* (London: Darton, Longman and Todd, 1986), pp. 82-85. The story is told in "The History of Mr. John Welsh," ascribed to James Kirkton, in *Select Biographies*, W. K. Tweedie, ed. (Edinburgh: Woodrow Society, 1845), Vol. 1, pp. 35ff.
10. William Booth, *The General's Letters 1885* (London: Salvationist Publishing and Supplies, 1886), pp. 82,83.
11. See Karl A. Olsson, *By One Spirit* (Chicago: Covenant Press, 1962), pp. 6068.
12. Kelsey, *Healing and Christianity*.
13. J. Sidlow Baxter, *Divine Healing of the Body* (Grand Rapids, MI: Zondervan Publishing House, 1979).
14. John Wimber with Kevin Springer, *Power Evangelism* (San Francisco: Harper and Row, 1986).
15. Gardner, *Healing Miracles*.
16. John Gunstone, *Healing Power* (Ann Arbor, MI: Servant Books, 1987).
17. Lewis B. Smedes, "On Reverence for Life and Discernment of Reality," *The Reformed Journal*, July 1987, p. 18.
18. Charles H. Kraft, "Worldview and Bible Translation," *Notes on Anthropology*, Summer Institute of Linguistics, June-Sept. 1986, p. 47.
19. Colin Brown, *That You May Believe* (Grand Rapids, MI: Wm. B. Eerdmans, 1985), p. 33.
20. Rex Gardner, "Miracles of Healing in Anglo-Celtic Northumbria as Recorded by the Venerable Bede and His Contemporaries: A Reappraisal in the Light of Twentieth Century Experience," *British Medical Journal*, Vol. 287, 1983, offprint p. 6.

21. Paul G. Hiebert, "The Flaw of the Excluded Middle," *Missiology: An International Review*, Vol. X, No. 1, Jan. 1982, p. 35.
22. Paul Brand with Philip Yancey, "A Surgeon's View of Divine Healing," *Christianity Today*, Nov. 25, 1983, p. 15.
23. Paul G. Hiebert, "A Conflict of World Views," *Together*, July-Sept. 1984, p. 23.
24. Jack MacDonald, "Stance," *TEAM Horizons*, Nov./Dec. 1982, p. 15.
25. Alan Tippett, *Introduction to Missiology* (Pasadena, CA: William Carey Library, 1987), p. 83.
26. Timothy M. Warner, "Encounter with Demon Power," *Trinity World Forum*, Winter 1981, p. 4.
27. Ibid.
28. Timothy M. Warner, "Power Encounter in Evangelism," *Trinity World Forum*, Winter 1985, p. 2.

SEVEN

LET'S BELIEVE THE WORKS OF JESUS

The central issue we have dealt with in the last two chapters is the passing of the power. If Jesus passed the power to His disciples and they passed it on to succeeding generations of Christians, we should be seeing it today. But whether we see it today or not largely depends on our worldview, as I have pointed out.

Believing is seeing. Jesus said of the skeptics in His day that even if someone rose from the dead, they would not be persuaded (see Luke 16:31). They could not see it because they did not believe.

So let's believe. Let's believe that Jesus will keep His promise that "the works that I do he will do also" (John 14:12). Without believing that, it will be difficult, if not impossible, to have a significant healing ministry in your church. Let's go to work on our worldview and try to bring our "reality" somewhat nearer to God's REALITY as we find it described in the Bible.

I realize that Jesus also said, "and greater works than these he will do" (v. 12). Many Christians today stumble at this phrase. For example, Colin Brown represents the thinking of many when he says that we have no biblical evidence that "supports the interpretation of this passage as a promise to do greater physical miracles." He is more comfortable in understanding Jesus to mean that His followers would extend their geographical boundaries and see conviction of sin and forgiveness, judgment, salvation and eternal life.[1]

My recommendation is that in order to avoid potential hassle, which will just divert us from our main task, let's put aside claims to greater works for the time being. Let's simply focus on doing the same works that Jesus did, or at least approaching them as nearly as possible. I have already explained why, given Jesus' unique relationship to the Father, we cannot expect to duplicate His ministry either in quantity or quality.

If we can't believe in greater works, can we at least believe in the same works? I hope so, because if we do, we will be able to look around today's world and see the same kinds of things that excited the people in Israel during the days of Jesus' ministry. We will see people today who are all amazed at the majesty of God (see Luke 9:43). We may only believe a little at first, but the more we see, the more we believe, and the more we believe, the more we see.

CONTEMPORARY SIGNS AND WONDERS

The works of the Father are so plentiful today that it is

difficult to classify them. But I am going to attempt to describe seven categories of contemporary signs and wonders that I believe will serve to build our faith. One of the steps toward starting a healing ministry in your church is to grasp something of the wondrous works of God in other places. I have chosen as examples the gift of language, nature miracles, filling teeth, spiritual transportation, multiplying food, creating new organs and raising the dead.

The Gift of Language

Those who object to the "greater works" teaching frequently point out that Jesus' disciples themselves did nothing greater than Jesus did. This may be true, depending on the meaning attached to *greater*. But I think it is at least significant that the first miracle done through the apostles after Jesus left them on their own was something that Jesus Himself never did, so far as we know. They shared the gospel message in at least 15 foreign languages they had never learned. The result? The people in Jerusalem who heard them on that first day of Pentecost "were all amazed and marveled." They asked, "How is it that we hear, each in our own language in which we were born?" (Acts 2:7,8).

This was the first time, but not the last. We read in Alban Butler's *The Lives of the Fathers, Martyrs, and Other Saints* that Dominican preacher Vincent Ferrer in the early 1400s was perfectly understood by Greeks, Germans, Sardes, Hungarians and others even though he had never learned a language other than his mother tongue of Valencian, except for a little Latin and Hebrew.[2]

While that one may be a bit difficult to double-check,

a similar case was closer to home. In 1985 I had the privilege of meeting a remarkable young missionary couple named James and Jaime Thomas. Soon after they were married some years ago they went to Argentina under Maranatha Ministries. Neither James nor Jaime had learned any Spanish while growing up in Kentucky. James had enrolled in a Spanish course in high school, but he was doing so poorly that he dropped it so as not to lower his grade point average.

When they arrived in Cordoba, Argentina, they began planting a church near the university campus by using interpreters. God blessed the ministry, and a small church was soon underway. At one point James invited a Puerto Rican Pentecostal evangelist, Ben Soto, to speak in a Sunday evening service. About 150 people were present. Soto, a dynamic speaker, was preaching fervently in Spanish when all of a sudden he stopped. The silence startled the congregation. They thought something had happened to the preacher.

But Soto was all right. In a few moments he said, in English, "James and Jaime, God has just told me that he is going to give you the gift of Spanish." He invited them to come up front, laid on his hands and blessed what God was doing. Then he said, "James, you take over," and he sat down. James was stunned and confused. He hadn't felt anything special during Ben Soto's prayer. So he instinctively called for his interpreter. But Soto insisted that he do it on his own in Spanish.

James reluctantly picked up the list of announcements he had written out in English, and began slowly, "En . . . esta . . . semana . . . vamos . . . a . . ." and proceeded to break into fluent Spanish, spoken with an Argentine accent. From that moment he has spoken Spanish like a native and written it with correct grammar, spelling and even accent marks. Not only that, but when God more recently called them to Guatemala, James found himself speaking immediately with a Guatemalan accent. He demonstrated to me (I am fluent in Spanish) how he could also speak the dialects of Honduras, Venezuela and Mexico. That would be equivalent to me switching my English accent at will from California to Kentucky to New England to Australia to Ireland.

Meanwhile, before Ben Soto came, Jaime had learned even less Spanish than her husband. She told me that she was so terrified when facing someone with whom she could not communicate that she would not even answer a knock at the door of her house. But after Soto's prayer, some women began to ask her questions in Spanish and she found herself answering them comfortably and fluently. For some reason, God did not give her a native accent, but she speaks well, although with an American accent.

I am in correspondence with Stella Bosworth, who has been a missionary to Africa for over 30 years. Her mother, Ethel Raath, a South African, knew a few words of pigeon Zulu, but that was all. In 1935 she and her husband were assigned to do government work in Transkei, a Zulu area, and when they arrived some Zulu Christians asked them to begin services for them. Mrs. Raath felt that God was calling her to minister and pray in Zulu, so she decided to ask Him for the language. She gathered the Zulu Christians, knelt down, placed the Zulu Bible on her head, and they prayed for her to speak Zulu. From the time she got up from her knees she could speak, read and write Zulu fluently. She became her husband's chief interpreter. Like James Thomas, God gave her a perfect Zulu accent so that they call her "the white Zulu."

I am also in correspondence with Norman Bonner, a

retired Wesleyan missionary to Haiti, and later among the Zulus as well. While in Haiti as a new missionary he had been studying French, intentionally postponing the study of Creole. But, finding himself in a situation one day when he felt he needed to preach in Creole, he specifically asked God for the language. From that time on he could preach fluently in Creole and interpret for visiting evangelists. One evangelist said, "I would give ten thousand dollars for your knowledge of Creole."

Jon and Cher Cadd, who fly with Mission Aviation Fellowship in Zimbabwe, tell of how a Zimbabwean interpreter received the Vidoma language. In his book *Bruchko*, Bruce Olson describes how, in Colombia, Motilone Indian evangelists were given the Yuko language, a dialect quite different from their native tongue.[3] Whether those involved in these two cases continued to speak the new language I do not know.

Stories like this highlight God's power, but they must not lead us to presumption. God sometimes works this way, but I suppose that both now and in the future some 99.9 percent of new missionaries will still have to learn languages like my wife and I learned Spanish—the old-fashioned way. Nevertheless, let's be open to God's surprises and accept them with gratitude.

Nature Miracles

While Jesus, so far as we know, never spoke in languages He did not learn, He did still the storm. The Father gave Him authority over nature at that point. How many other storms He stilled, we are not told. It is safe to assume, however, that in His lifetime He passed through many storms that He had to endure like everyone else, because the Father did not choose to still them. The apostle Paul did not still the storm in which he was shipwrecked. In fact God told him that the storm would wreck the boat but that no one on it would die (see Acts 27:9-44). Sometimes God lets nature take its course; sometimes He intervenes miraculously.

Do Christians, using the power that was given to Jesus, take authority over nature today? At times they do. For example, the Christian Surfing Association is a group of evangelists who witness to Southern California surfers, mostly through sponsoring surfing contests. A contest was recently scheduled for Stone Steps near San Diego, but it had been months since that beach had enjoyed acceptable surf and as the day approached, the outlook was glum. So Mark Curtis, the president, and his team gathered the night before and asked God for surf. The next day saw some of the best waves of the year. A lifeguard they were witnessing to said, "You guys must have connections upstairs because this place hasn't broken in over a year."[4]

In Colombia the Nevado de Ruiz volcano erupted in 1985 and virtually wiped out the town of Armero. Of a population of 25,000, no less than 22,000 were dead or missing. But the Church of God (Cleveland, TN) reports that none of their churches were destroyed nor were any believers injured. In one Assemblies of God church, the pastor's wife and baby were alone, right in the pathway of the mud that was burying the town. But the mud flow divided just before it came to the church and merged again on the other side as if some supernatural power were protecting them.

Kalimantan in 1982 had been suffering a four months' drought. Huge brush fires were burning out of control. Missionary Fred Voightmann reports that a Christian school was directly in the path of the flames, which were higher than the school buildings as they approached. All the buildings were flammable, some made of wood and some of straw. The teachers and 47 junior-high-age children gathered in the courtyard, joined hands in a circle and prayed God's protection. The fire roared to within a few feet of the buildings, jumped the compound and burned several hundred acres on the other side.

I began praying in generalities, but I soon felt a strong presence of the Holy Spirit, which I recognized as a special anointing.

While running for president, Pat Robertson was occasionally criticized, even ridiculed by some, for claiming that in 1985 his prayer helped turn Hurricane Gloria around and keep it from destroying his headquarters in Virginia Beach, Virginia. The accounts were especially interesting to me because one year previously I was involved in a similar prayer.

I was in Stuttgart, Germany in September 1984 at a meeting of the Lausanne Committee for World Evangelization (L.C.W.E). News began to come over the English language Armed Forces Network that the most severe hurricane of the season, Diana, was approaching the North Carolina coast, expected to move inland rapidly with great destructive force. Leighton Ford, president of L.C.W.E., owned a home right in the anticipated path of the storm. He and his wife, Jean, who was with him, expressed their fears that they might lose everything.

As I recall, we received word that Diana was about to cross the coast at Cape Fear, North Carolina, about 10:30 A.M. Stuttgart time. The plenary committee was in session under the direction of Kirsti Mosvold of Norway. She stopped the meeting, gave the news of the storm and suggested we pause for prayer. "Peter Wagner," she said, "will you lead us?"

I got on my feet slowly because I had not been prepared for such an event. I began praying in generalities, but I soon felt a strong presence of the Holy Spirit, which I recognized as a special anointing. I sensed that God was telling me to still the storm. The magnitude of the risk flashed through my mind. Here were some 100 of the top evangelical leaders from around the globe. No fewer than five or six bishops were among them. They were listening to me intently. What if I tell the storm to stop and nothing happens? What if it wasn't really God speaking to me?

But I decided to go for it. I found myself praying in a loud voice with uncharacteristic authority. I cited the power that flowed through Jesus to still the storm on Lake Galilee. I said that if Jesus could do it then, we can do it now. I spoke directly to Hurricane Diana, took authority over it, and told it to stop in the name of Jesus. I asked the Lord to protect Leighton Ford's property against any damage. Then I sat down and the meeting went on.

Right after lunch I turned my radio to the 1:00 P.M. Armed Forces News broadcast. The headline item was that Hurricane Diana had suddenly stopped short of the coast. A subsequent interview with Robert C. Sheets of the National Hurricane Center in Miami revealed that at the time of the prayer the hurricane was a "category 3" storm, that a drastic change took place, and it was downgraded to "category 1" before it finally did move ashore. Leighton Ford's property suffered no damage.

I will be the first to admit that the dramatic changes

of events in the surf or the volcano or the fire or the hurricane could be ascribed to inexplicable quirks of nature. But to someone who believes, they could also be ascribed to powerful prayer (not only my own, but undoubtedly the prayers of others as well) and the direct intervention of the hand of God. I want to be one who believes.

Filling Teeth

In chapter 3 I reported the great growth of churches in Argentina through power evangelism and mentioned that the miraculous filling of teeth was common there. I must confess that when they first began telling me about it I was more than a bit skeptical. For some strange reason I could feel much more comfortable about God's healing cancer than I could about filling teeth. I was hearing stories about gold fillings, silver fillings and white fillings. Some were reported to have imprints of the cross in them. Some would spit out the old fillings while others were transformed the way they were. There were reports of bridges falling out and being replaced by teeth, as well as new teeth growing in where they had previously been extracted.

I didn't know if God was doing this in places other than Argentina until I came across two other references to the phenomenon. My first sense of consolation came when both authors confessed, as I did, a sense of skepticism.

In his classic book *Healing*, Francis MacNutt saves one story for an epilogue because he was afraid that it would be a bit too much for the average reader to believe and he didn't want to lose readers before they finished the book. He calls it "The Story of the Three

Indians," and challenges the readers to test their credulity. To make a long story short, Lucy Keeble, a Sioux, heard her son complain of a toothache. He suggested that they go to a nearby healing service. Seven of his teeth were filled. The other was a young Sioux named Nancy. She was neither a Christian nor disposed to being prayed for even though she had severe cavities and had not been to a dentist. The preacher prayed for her anyway; her upper teeth were filled with gold and her lower teeth with silver. And all this happened in Minneapolis, not in Buenos Aires.[5]

Rex Gardner, the British physician, includes a chapter in his excellent book *Healing Miracles*, which he calls "God's Strange Work." It deals mostly with filling teeth. In the introduction to the chapter, he admits that some of his respected friends strongly advised him to omit the chapter. But he castigates himself for tending to feel "embarrassed when God oversteps the mark."[6]

Gardner tells MacNutt's story, then describes some research he did on similar reports from Chile. It began with an article in *Crusade* magazine published in 1976 by John Pridemore who had just visited Chile. He reports looking into several mouths with a flashlight after a healing service and says, "I know what I see is a miracle . . . these teeth have been filled. And the filling has the form of a silver cross set in each tooth."[7] Gardner followed this up with extended contact with three individuals who were not, as he says, "exuberant gullible witnesses:" Bill Maxwell, a physician, his trained nurse wife and Kath Clark, an Anglican missionary. Firsthand examinations by all three confirmed that teeth had been filled without the help of a dentist. Are they reliable stories? Gardner says, "Of their veracity I have no doubt."[8]

While I was skeptical about the miraculous filling of

teeth, I no longer am. In fact I must admit that the last time I went to Argentina I harbored a secret desire that some of my own teeth which, although in good repair on the surface are a disaster area underneath, would be replaced. They weren't.

Spiritual Transportation

Luke tells the story of an angry crowd in Nazareth that had decided to kill Jesus by pushing Him over a cliff. But He escaped by "passing through the midst of them" (4:30). We are not told how He got through, but it could have been that God bypassed the usual restrictions of time and space and supernaturally transported His body to another place. This is not beyond possibility because it apparently is exactly what did happen to Philip after he baptized the Ethiopian eunuch: "the Spirit of the Lord caught Philip away, so that the eunuch saw him no more" (Acts 8:39).

Admittedly, my research has not uncovered many contemporary examples of spiritual transportation. I do have a rather remarkable anecdote about Oklahoma oil magnate Al Wheeler who claimed to be transported from Tulsa to Uganda and back. In Uganda he witnessed to an old witch doctor and his family. The experience was reportedly confirmed by some thick gumbo mud on his shoes, which he had analyzed in a soils lab. It had come from no place in mid-America, but was characteristic of East Africa. Later, in the U.S., he met the son of the witch doctor, they immediately recognized each other, and the African exclaimed that he had seen Wheeler in his village in Uganda. I am in correspondence with Wheeler's wife, Marilyn, who assures me that her late husband was a credible, relatively unemotional man, who moved freely in high circles of business and government where his credulity was not a point of issue.

A more widely publicized account comes from the personal testimony of the late David du Plessis, known worldwide as Mr. Pentecost, and for whom Fuller Seminary's DuPlessis Center for Christian Spirituality is named. The event, says DuPlessis, was "so powerful and so alien to our natural ways of life" that he refrained from speaking about it for many years lest he be misunderstood.[9]

He was ministering to two men in Ladybrand, South Africa when a word from God came to him that he was needed immediately in the house of a brother who had been demonized. He told the two others that he would run and they could come later. The house was about a mile away. Then "it all happened in two or three seconds." DuPlessis went through the gate, heard it click behind him, and "that's all I remember. When I lifted my foot to run, I put it down at the front door of the man's house."[10]

DuPlessis cast out the demon and was ministering to the man. His two friends showed up 20 minutes later and were astounded to discover that DuPlessis had already been there for 20 minutes. "It was then I realized," says DuPlessis, "I must have been transported by the Holy Spirit."[11]

After telling his own story, DuPlessis relates another case of a Basuto man who was transported 15 miles from one mountain peak to another, also to cast out some demons. Then he was transported back.[12]

Multiplying Food

On one occasion Jesus fed 5,000 people with five loaves

of bread and two fish (see Matt. 14:15-21). On another he fed 4,000 with seven loaves of bread and a few fish (see 15:32-39). While there may not be many known cases of spiritual transportation, instances of food being multiplied are fairly common.

Rebecca Chao, for example, reports that on her trips to visit the house churches in China she frequently hears stories of food multiplying. The specifics vary, she says, "but in each case God did not let His believers go hungry."[13] My friend Paul Landrey tells of a Christian convention he attended in India where bananas were multiplied. Kurt Koch documents the multiplication of meat, rice and bananas in Indonesia. He tells of an evangelistic team of 15 that was given 9 bananas. They carried them for a distance, and when they stopped to eat there was one banana for each team member.[14]

Multiplication of food is not just a modern-day phenomenon. Rex Gardner cites a case of flour being multiplied in an orphanage in nineteenth-century France.[15] Herbert Thurston, S.J. does an objective study of the multiplications of food in his book *The Physical Phenomena of Mysticism*, and concludes, "It would be an endless task to try to compile a list of devout people in whose lives such multiplications of food are recorded."[16] The beatification investigations of many of the Roman Catholic saints have frequently uncovered such incidents.

Because of its fairly wide publicity and frequency of occurrence, the multiplication of food under the ministry of Father Richard "Rick" Thomas in El Paso, Texas is one of the best known examples in the U.S. It began on Christmas of 1972. Through a Bible study in a youth center, Rick Thomas was impressed by the Lord to serve a Christmas dinner at the garbage dump in Juarez, Mexico. The guests were to be the poorest of the poor—those who live as scavengers at the dump. They prepared 120 Mexican burritos with tamales, a ham,

I don't recall any miracle stories from the New Testament that specifically tell of new organs or new bodily members being created . . . but . . . there are some examples of new organs being created today.

chocolate milk and some fruit. The food might possibly have stretched for 150, but 300 showed up. Miraculously, not only did the food reach, but each person had a slice of ham as thick as their hand. Thomas reports, "All ate their fill and many took bags of groceries away with them. And there was still more than enough."[17] In fact, they left food at three orphanages on the way home.

In a book length study of Thomas' ministry in El Paso, Rene Laurentin painstakingly chronicles subsequent multiplication of food: multiplication of flour, December 1975; multiplication of grapes, July 1977; distribution of avocados and tortillas, December 1977; distribution of canned milk, January 1978; distribution of grapes, July 1979; abnormal filling of sacks with squash, April 1980.[18]

Even nearer to home, a ham was multiplied through one of the members of my Lake Avenue Congregational Church 120 Fellowship Sunday School class. Our class regularly provides meals for the homeless at local shelters. In this case, Celeste Coleman, who coordinates this ministry for us, had asked another class member to deliver ham enough for 86 people to the Fair Oaks Family Shelter. But signals were somehow crossed and when Celeste arrived to prepare and serve the meal, she discovered that only an eight-pound canned ham had been delivered. She laid hands on the ham and asked God to bless it to all who were there. She doesn't know whether it was in the slicing or the serving or both, but all 86 people ate their fill of ham and there was some left over.

Creating New Organs

I don't recall any miracle stories from the New Testament that specifically tell of new organs or new bodily members being created. Perhaps the fingers and toes of some of the cleansed lepers were restored, but details are not given. The man born blind possibly received new eyes or optic nerves. Jesus restored an ear that Peter had cut off, but we do not know whether he reattached the old ear or created a new one (see Luke 22:50,51). At any rate, there are some examples of new organs being created today.

The first I heard of such things happening was through my friend Omar Cabrera of Argentina. He reported a six-year-old girl who had one lung removed through surgery and the lung was later replaced through prayer. In another case a little boy born without ears was said to have both ears pop out with a snap, like bubble gum, at one of Cabrera's meetings. I recall that John Wimber phoned me the day after they had finished a signs and wonders conference in Seattle to tell me that with several physicians looking on a woman's toe had grown out.

All this was fascinating to me, but it became more than that in February of 1987. The son and daughter-in-law of our School of World Mission dean, Paul Pierson, had made an appointment with me to pray for their son. The young couple, Steve and Sara Pierson, had spent some time doing social work in Guatemala and while there they had adopted a Guatemalan boy named Christian who had been born with no ears. He had been fitted with a high-tech hearing device, which looks like Sony Walkman earphones, and with that he could hear some and he had learned to speak. But when he came into my seminary office he had only a tiny nub on each side of his head with no ear canals. He also was partially blind in the left eye.

It looked so hopeless that I confess I had very little faith when I laid hands on his head and then his left eye and asked God to heal him in Jesus' name. There was no evidence of anything happening, so I tried to encourage Chris and his parents as much as I could and they left. About a half hour later when they were going into Marie Callender's restaurant, Sara said to Steve, "Do you see what I see?" He admitted that he had already seen it, but wasn't going to say anything. The ears had started to grow.

The next morning they were driving down the street when Chris said, "Mommie, what does b-a-k-e-r-y spell?" Sara said, "You can't see that sign, you don't have your contact lens." But he did see it. He said, "Ever since Dr. Wagner prayed for my eye it has been burning, and I can see better now."

Chris's ears aren't perfect yet. But he does have small ears on both sides, complete with ear canals. He still needs the help of the hearing device, but plans to put him in a special school have now been changed.

Some frosting on the cake was added four months later when Steve and Sara brought Chris in for another session of prayer. Sara mentioned that women on both sides of her family had a condition of the upper spine that caused them to bend forward. She was concerned because it was becoming more difficult to breathe, she had chronic back pain, and furthermore it didn't look good. Sara had been a beauty queen in her hometown of Fresno, California. Would I pray for that also?

I was delighted to. George Eckart, the director of the prayer/healing team in my 120 Fellowship Sunday School class, was with me so we prayed as a team. We discovered a short leg, and it responded instantly to prayer. Then as we began to pray for her back, the Holy Spirit came upon her visibly. She went into something like a trance and began to shake, even though she was standing the whole time. George and I felt the bones and muscles of her back and shoulders moving under our hands, and her spine became perfectly straight. It was so noticeable that a relative who saw her the next day asked her if she had started wearing a new back brace. She gained three quarters of an inch in height. She later wrote, "This has been an amazing change in my physical appearance and my spiritual life."

But that's not all. While the Holy Spirit was resting on Sara, Steve was seated over on the other side of the room. The Spirit of God moved on him in an uncharacteristic way and prompted him to pray that Sara would conceive and have a child. For several years they had wanted a biological child, but they were beginning to despair. Sure enough, it happened almost immediately, and as I write this her pregnancy is well-advanced and everything is normal.

Raising the Dead

Many people consider raising Lazarus from the dead

after four days as Jesus' most dramatic miracle. Therefore it is predictable that that those who question
whether the works that Jesus did are still being done
today will eventually play, as Rex Gardner calls it, "their
trump card" and say: "If this is so, if those fabulous
promises are still true as you say, then where are the
cases of raising the dead?"[19]

Not long ago I was having what I felt was a fairly positive discussion of healing with an internationally
respected theologian until the subject of raising the
dead came up. He left no doubt as to his position. He
said, "There—that is where I draw the line. Healing, yes.
Casting out demons, perhaps. I'm willing to talk about
those things, but not raising the dead. That is an extre-
mism which I cannot tolerate."

I may not have been quite as blunt, but until fairly
recently I had doubts about the possibility of truly dead
people coming back to life nowadays. My presupposi-
tion was that death is irreversible and that any apparent
raising of the dead must be explained by the fact that
the person was never truly dead, but perhaps in some
comatose state of suspended animation.

A dramatic event in my own Lake Avenue Congregational Church helped me to reexamine that presupposi-
tion. Sara Cadenhead, a young mother who attended
our church, was out in the backyard of her home just
before Thanksgiving 1982. She suddenly noticed that
her 12-month-old son, John Eric, had disappeared from
sight some time ago. Her worst fears were realized when
she found him face down floating in the swimming pool.
Pulling him out, she was horrified to find that he had
stopped breathing and turned blue. She called the para-
medics who examined him, but too late. Paramedic
Mark Nelson declared him "clinically dead."[20] Meanwhile

a police patrol car had stopped by and the officer volunteered to take the boy to the Huntington Hospital. So Sara picked him up and they went to the emergency room.

Coincidentally, the two pediatricians who took the case, Richard Johnson and William Sears, were both members of Lake Avenue Congregational Church. My wife, Doris, took a special interest in the case. She interviewed the pediatricians. She received permission from Sara Cadenhead to examine the medical records. With the documentation she assembled, she wrote the story up for *Christian Life* magazine (Sept. 1983).

As it turned out, John Eric had been without vital signs for a minimum of 40 minutes, probably more. Medication did restore some reflex heart motion, but it was so artificial that the doctor wrote on the medical instructions, "Do not resuscitate."

Fortunately for Sara and John Eric, God didn't get that message. A call had gone in to a local Christian television studio, Trinity Broadcasting Network (TBN), and special prayer went up. Late that night Sara went back to the hospital in obedience to a word from the Lord, took the body in her arms, and began to rub it with hospital lotion. After several hours, consciousness began to return to the body, and soon John Eric opened his eyes and pulled the glasses off a nurse.

The neurologists predicted 100-percent brain damage, and said John Eric would probably be a vegetable. But in a week he was out of the hospital and soon he was perfectly normal in every way. The medical personnel at the hospital nicknamed him Baby Lazarus. The local daily newspaper the *Pasadena Star News* featured the story, complete with pictures, on the front page under the headline: "MIRACLE."[21] Sara and John Eric attended my Sunday School class for a time, so we got to know them well.

The facts are well documented. But the interpretation of the facts will depend on the observer's worldview. Believing is seeing. For those who have decided that death is irreversible, something other than miraculous raising of the dead happened to John Eric.

THE INDONESIAN REVIVAL

These issues were debated during and after the well-known Indonesian revival, which began in 1965 and ran into the early '70s. Numerous stories of New Testament level signs and wonders were coming out of Indonesia in those days, including some about dead people being raised.

The news was so exciting that many Christian leaders flew to Indonesia to see for themselves. One of them was missiologist George W. Peters of Dallas Theological Seminary. We know more about Peter's visit than some of the others because he reports his findings in his book *Indonesian Revival*. In it, he strongly asserts his belief in a sovereign, miracle-working God. He affirms that if God chooses to do so, He can perform miracles today just as He did in the New Testament times.

George Peters also insists that we are to test the spirits, so he decided to put the Indonesia stories to the test. He read widely, traveled extensively and did numerous interviews. His conclusion: "I do not doubt that God is able to raise the dead, but I seriously question that He did so in Timor. In fact, I am convinced that it did not happen." He then goes on to explain that "according to *their usage* of the word *death*, and their concept of *death*, they had experienced resuscitation." But "According to my concept of death, no such miracles happened."[22]

What was the Indonesian concept of death? Was it really that far from ours?

One of the Indonesian leaders of the revival was Mel Tari, who has also recorded his observations in *Like a Mighty Wind*. In it we read that Tari's small ministry team had been called to a funeral in the village of Amfoang to console the grieving family. The man had been dead for two days and with no embalming was decomposing rapidly. Tari says, "In our tropical country, when you're dead six hours you start to decay. But after two days—oh, I tell you, you couldn't stand within 100 feet of him. You smelled that smell and it was awful."[23] I will admit that different cultures see death in different ways, but if Tari's description is accurate, it sounds like a cross-culturally valid example of death.

In the middle of the funeral, God told Tari and his team to stand around the corpse and sing songs until the man was raised from the dead. So, even though the stench was making them sick, they obeyed. On the sixth song the corpse began to move its toes. By the end of the eighth song he was awake and smiling. This resulted in some dramatic power evangelism, and eventually, Tari reports, 21,000 people in the area came to know Jesus Christ through the man's testimony.

But, since believing is seeing, some are not even convinced by this case. Others are. Kurt Koch also went to Indonesia to investigate. He says, "I too, doubted the reports that were coming out of the revival area." But after seeing for himself, he says, "Today I can doubt them no more since I have actually spoken with the leaders of the revival themselves."[24] He then goes on to document several cases of the dead being raised. At about that same time Don Crawford was sent by Ken Taylor of Tyndale House to report on the revival. He affirms in his book that "Faith healing, demon purging, and resurrection from the dead are all a part of the religious phenomena of Indonesia."[25]

As I have traveled to many areas of the world since becoming a part of the third wave, I have made it a point to inquire about the dead being raised, and I have heard several firsthand reports as well as many other secondhand reports. People I respect such as Daisy Osborne of Tulsa, Oklahoma and Benson Idahosa of Benin City, Nigeria and Ki Dong Kim of Seoul, Korea and others have themselves been used to bring dead people back to life. My good friend, Paul Yonggi Cho, sat in my own living room not long ago and told a group of missiologists how God had used him to raise his own son, Samuel, from the dead.

Is it always God's will to raise the dead? Of course not. I like the response of an Indonesian leader who had been used to raise 12 people from the dead to a question posed by Lester Sumrall: "How do you raise the dead?"

He said, "We say a simple prayer: 'Lord, has this person lived out his days that You ordained?' . . . . If the Lord says yes, we bury the body. If the Lord says no, we say, 'We'll stop that right now. Death, hear us. We speak to you in the name of the glorious Son of God Who rose from the dead. Death, you leave him now.' His life returns."[26]

This brings us back to our basic guideline: If we do the works that Jesus did, we, like Jesus, will only do what we see the Father doing. We ourselves do not raise the dead or multiply food or fill teeth or create new organs. The Father does. But we can become channels for the Father to do these things, according to His will, by the power of the Holy Spirit. That's what the third wave is all about.

Notes ———————————————————————————

1. Colin Brown, *That You May Believe* (Grand Rapids, MI: Wm B. Eerdmans Pub. Co., 1985), pp. 198,199.
2. Alban Butler, *The Lives of the Fathers, Martyrs, and Other Principal Saints* (New York: D. & J. Sadlier & Co., n.d.), Vol. II, p. 33.
3. Bruce Olson, *Bruchko* (Carol Stream, IL: Creation House, 1978), pp. 159-161.
4. Eric Bailey, "Christian Surfers Rely on Power of Waves to Spread the Gospel," *Los Angeles Times*, Jan. 17, 1987, II:4.
5. Francis MacNutt, *Healing* (Notre Dame, IN: Ave Maria Press, 1974), pp. 327-333.
6. Rex Gardner, *Healing Miracles* (London: Darton, Longman and Todd, 1986), p. 175.
7. Ibid., p. 178.
8. Ibid., p. 181.
9. David duPlessis, *A Man Called Mr. Pentecost* (Plainfield, NJ: Logos International, 1977), p. 82.
10. Ibid., p. 84.
11. Ibid., p. 86.
12. Ibid., pp. 86,87.
13. Rebecca Chao, "Can Miracles Ever Become Commonplace?" *China and the Church Today*, 1981, p. 20.
14. Kurt Koch, *The Revival in Indonesia* (Grand Rapids, MI: Kregal Publications, 1972), p. 134.
15. Gardner, *Healing Miracles*, p. 13.
16. Herbert Thurston, S.J., *The Physical Phenomena of Mysticism* (Chicago: Henry Regnery Co., 1952), p. 394. Reference from Rene Laurentin, Miracles in El Paso? (Ann Arbor, MI: Servant Books, 1982), p. 100.
17. Rick Thomas, "Christmas at the Dump," *Charisma*, Dec. 1985, p. 55.
18. Laurentin, *Miracles in El Paso?* pp. 96,97.
19. Gardner, *Healing Miracles*, p. 137.
20. Brandon Bailey, "Miracle: One can happen—ask Buzzy's Mom" *Pasadena Star News*, Pasadena, CA, Dec. 12, 1982, p. 1.
21. Ibid.
22. George W. Peters, *Indonesia Revival* (Grand Rapids, MI: Zondervan Publishing House, 1973), pp. 80,83.
23. Mel Tari, *Like a Mighty Wind* (Carol Stream, IL: Creation House, 1971), p. 66.
24. Koch, *Revival in Indonesia*, p. 130.
25. Don Crawford, *Miracles in Indonesia* (Wheaton, IL: Tyndale House, 1972), p. 84.
26. Lester Sumrall, *Faith to Change the World* (Tulsa, OK: Harrison House, 1984), p. 69.

EIGHT

DEMONS AT HOME AND ABROAD

I am fully cognizant of the risk involved in including a chapter on demons in this book. I haven't done much writing on the subject previously, and the few times I have tried it landed me in one of the biggest hassles I can remember with some of my colleagues around Fuller Seminary. They tacked my articles up on the campus Board of Declaration, where they became the focal point of strenuous debate. The seminary president invited me, along with my dean, to his office to explain my position. I can honestly say that up to that point I had been totally naive about how edgy some Christian leaders could be on the matter. Today I am better informed.

But an even higher potential risk is becoming the object of demonic attacks. As I write this my personal intercessors are on special assignment, intensifying their usual prayer ministry on my behalf. Others have warned us of the dangers. Francis MacNutt, for example, mentions that he considered leaving out his chapter on deliverance because it is so controversial.[1] Michael

> *As I write this my personal intercessors are on special assignment, intensifying their usual prayer ministry on my behalf.*

Green says his book *I Believe in Satan's Downfall* was not "an easy or an enjoyable book to write."[2] He also mentions that C. S. Lewis was said to have felt very much the same when he wrote his classic *Screwtape Letters*. If they are susceptible, so much more am I.

BEING READY

Anyone who begins a healing ministry needs to do so with the realization that sooner or later they will probably be confronted with demons. For one thing, the four major areas of healing in general include spiritual healing, physical healing, emotional healing and, of course, demonization. For another, even when someone is not dealing directly with the demonized but doing other works of the Father, satanic opposition is often stirred up.

So even though including a chapter on demons involves a risk, I feel it would be an even greater risk to have people read a book on the third wave, begin to pray for the sick, and remain ignorant of possible attacks from the enemy who "walks about like a roaring lion, seeking whom he may devour" (1 Pet. 5:8). Peter says that in order to avoid the danger, we must "be sober, be vigilant" (v. 8). And the recommended way to deal with the enemy is to "resist him" (v. 9). The Bible never says that the best way to handle the devil is to ignore him.

I do not intend to treat the subject of demons and spiritual warfare exhaustively. That would require a book, not a chapter. Furthermore, several good books on the subject are currently available, such as Michael Green's *I Believe in Satan's Downfall*, Mark Bubeck's *The Adversary and Overcoming the Adversary*, Michael Harper's *Spiritual Warfare*, C. Fred Dickason's *Demon Possession and the Christian* and others. I recommend serious reading in the area, but I also recommend seeking out those who have a deliverance ministry and learning from them.

While it is most advisable that people with experience be called on to deal with the demonic, it is also good for all of us to be ready at all times, for many Christian workers have suddenly found themselves in a situation where they have had to confront demons one-on-one, whether they like it or not. I recall hearing Paul Pierson, the dean of the Fuller School of World Mission, tell of his experience as a Presbyterian missionary in the jungles of western Brazil when he was brought face-to-face with a demonized girl in an isolated place. What did he do? Even though inexperienced, he found himself commanding the demon to leave in the name of Jesus, and it did. He was ready.

I was glad that my wife, Doris, was ready when it happened one afternoon in my seminary office. A woman had made a routine appointment for prayer, because she had a severe pain in her ankle. As I do at times, but not always, I asked her permission to anoint her with oil. The instant the oil touched her forehead, the demons manifested, screaming in loud voices. I knew at once what was happening, but I was ill-prepared to deal with it. All I could think of doing was to tell the demons to shut up, which I did in a very loud voice.

DORIS TAKES OVER

At that moment Doris, who works as my secretary just outside my office, came charging around the corner and immediately assumed control of the situation. She had just finished taking a four-week course on Ministering to the Demonized, taught by Carol Wimber and Gloria Thompson at Vineyard Christian Fellowship of Anaheim. I was totally astonished by her energy level, her poise, her complete self-control and the extraordinary authority in her voice. I, of course, soon recognized it as an anointing of the Holy Spirit, because she was doing and saying things I had never seen her do or say before. The whole event lasted over an hour. I soon discovered that I was not to be part of it, so I just stood to one side taking notes and holding the waste basket, which I shoved under the woman's mouth at opportune times.

The first thing Doris found out was that there were 10 demons in the woman. As soon as she got the name of each, out it would come. The woman's mouth would move and foam, and as Doris coaxed, the name would eventually be spoken. It was easy to tell when the woman was speaking and when the demon spoke. Each spirit that left choked her, and she roared violently as if vomiting, then spit up some slime.

The first one was a spirit of lust. The second was fear. The third was a spirit of death, which said it had entered when the woman was 15 years old and her mother had died. It told Doris that it was huge and could not leave, because it had no other place to go. The woman confirmed that she had long been deathly frightened of a seven-foot monster. But it left. The fourth was named Ugly and had persuaded the woman that her teeth were so ugly that she would avoid looking into a mirror. (Her teeth were normal.) The fifth was a spirit of false tongues. She had received what she thought was the gift of tongues three months previously, but every time she spoke in tongues, something would go from her stomach up her throat and choke her. As soon as that spirit came out, the woman burst out singing a praise song to Jesus in English. The sixth was a spirit of resentment, which had entered during a family crisis when she was 12 years old.

Doris's biggest battle was with the seventh, a spirit of anger. She said to it, "Are you the big one?" and it was. I was fascinated to observe that Doris knew exactly when they were lying, which they did frequently. Some gave her a good argument, but she always won. The spirit of anger violently shook the woman's head, then her neck, then one arm, then a foot, then her whole trunk, then her chest, then her eyes and, finally, her tongue, before it reluctantly came out. More noise was being generated through all of this than usually comes from a seminary professor's office, but an alert secretary outside knew precisely what was happening, and she kept everyone calm. A spirit of tiredness then came out after showing its power by almost putting the woman to sleep right then and there. That was followed by a spirit of rejection. The last one was a spirit of handicap, which would not let her lift her hands for a time until he left. Then she could lift her arms normally.

Doris counseled the woman, prayed with her, and she went on her way rejoicing. By then we had all forgotten about the pain in the ankle. Presumably it was healed.

SPIRITUAL WARFARE

One of the reasons I tell that story is to leave no doubt as to whether or not I think demons are real. I certainly do, and I believe that we are in warfare even though many Christians deny it or ignore it, which is almost as bad. I agree with John Wimber's prophetic words: "We wear our Christianity mainly for the admiration of each other—being a Christian has become fun and fashionable. When someone begins to remind us that there is spiritual war going on, we become uncomfortable—our frothy good time has been spoiled." That is undoubtedly why some react strongly against articles or chapters on demons, like this one. But, as Wimber says, "The fact is that whether or not we want to hear about it, we are in the midst of a war between God and Satan, which has been raging since the days of Adam and Eve."[3]

Just looking around at the world today should convince any and all that we are in spiritual warfare. Of course, many will look, but they won't see because, as I have mentioned several times, believing is seeing. So the first step in getting a grasp on what we have called the REALITY of spiritual warfare is to believe that demons are real.

It wasn't too long ago that my colleague, clinical psychologist Newton Malony, doubted whether demons were real. But, as a leading professor in Fuller's School of Psychology, he always has been vitally interested in integrating psychology with Christian doctrine, values and ministry. He is a careful scientist, who thoroughly examines all evidence available before coming to conclusions, especially when they involve a paradigm shift. But as he listened to, and at times became involved in, the signs and wonders debate at Fuller Seminary in the mid-'80s, he began to change his mind about demons.

Malony does not identify himself as a third-waver.

> *Recognizing that demons are active today*
> *... is a valuable asset in doing kingdom*
> *ministry.*

But now when he lectures, he tells his students that demons are real, and that when they appear, they need to be dealt with. In a recent address at the American Academy of Religion he listed four options for understanding mental illness as diseased (the medical model), deluded (the psychological model), depraved (the legal model) and demonized (the religious model), and affirms that none of the four should be ignored by mental health professionals. He recognizes that many do, in fact, ignore the possibility of demonization, but in his opinion, "the demonic cannot be so easily dismissed."[4]

Malony identifies specific symptoms of demonization to include altered states of consciousness, multiple personalities, speaking in cross-sex voice, blaspheming of religion, logic tight delusions, supernormal strength and rancid bodily odor. He suggests that Christian therapists move beyond their reluctance to recognize the demonic and look into "the viability of including the option of demonic possession among the alternative explanations of mental illness."[5] Malony now assists Professor Samuel Southard in teaching the course *CN571 Demonology and Mental Illness.*

Some use the term *demon possession*, while others shy away from it, feeling that it overstates the case. The biblical word *daimonizomenoi* is sometimes translated "to be possessed by a demon," as it is defined, for example, in Colin Brown's *The New International Dictionary of New Testament Theology.*[6] But most people I know who are regularly involved in deliverance ministries prefer the transliteration of the Greek, which comes into English as *demonized.* John Wimber, for example, says, "I do not believe that demons may own people absolutely while they still live on earth; even when demons gain a high degree of control, people are able to exercise a degree of free will that may lead to deliverance and salvation."[7] I am convinced that as long as we recognize that it comes in different degrees, the term *demonization* is the best one to use, because it carries the most accurate and pastorally sensitive message.

A SIGN OF THE KINGDOM

In chapter 4 I attempted to explain how the biblical teaching on the kingdom of God gives a framework for understanding third-wave type ministries today. Casting out demons is one of the signs of the presence of God's kingdom in the world today. Jesus said, "If I cast out demons with the finger of God, surely the kingdom of God has come upon you" (Luke 11:20). When Jesus first sent out the 12 apostles, "He gave them power over unclean spirits, to cast them out" (Matt. 10:1). He later sent out 70 disciples who, when they returned, said, "Lord, even the demons are subject to us in Your name" (Luke 10:17). The longer ending of Mark says, "And these signs will follow those who believe: In My name they will cast out demons" (Mark 16:17).

Recognizing that demons are active today, not only in some mentally ill persons but also in many other aspects of daily life, is a valuable asset in doing kingdom ministry. The kingdom of God has come to destroy the kingdom of Satan, and some of the resultant warfare is messy. In many parts of the world, as I pointed out a while ago, people live day in and day out in firsthand contact with evil spirits. Many of us may have a worldview with an "excluded middle," but they don't. In their minds the best gift that Jesus could bring to them would be power to defeat evil spirits. Forgiveness of sins is also important for them, but further down the agenda.

The Case of Brazil

Take Brazil, for example. Spiritism, which has as its main tenet bringing people into direct contact with the spirit world, is a national institution. It is reported that 70 percent of the Brazilian population frequents the more than 300,000 spiritist centers.[8] During soccer matches rival teams contract spiritist practitioners who work spells on each other. Spiritist healers perform surgery without anesthesia, pain or bleeding. Crowds of up to 250,000 pack the beaches of Praia Grande for the annual festival of the goddess of the sea. Some government officials regularly consult mediums before making important decisions.

The growth rate of Brazilian spiritism is frightening. Today's 70 percent represents an increase from only 8 percent 40 years ago. Roman Catholicism has been greatly weakened. Research has shown that only 2.5 percent of Brazilians look to priests or pastors for help these days because they consider them powerless to deal with the effects of magic spells.[9] Only Pentecostalism is able to match the growth of spiritism, chiefly because Pentecostals in general understand spiritual warfare and do not shy away from it. Free Methodist missionary C. Wesley King says, "In a real sense, spiritism and Pentecostals are locked in a spiritual battle for the soul of this nation."[10]

It is sad to hear a report from Valdemar Kroker that in Brazil the majority of evangelical groups take a position that "avoids as much as possible any contact with spiritism." I agree with Kroker, who says that "such an attitude of running away from reality is not tolerable in our day."[11] It certainly won't get the job of world evangelization done. Brazilian Pentecostal leader W. Robert McAlister says, "If a missionary can't cast out demons, he might as well go home."[12]

America Also?

Some Americans may take comfort in the fact that Brazil is so far away. If so, they need to have a closer look at our own country. A recent marketing survey showed that in one year approximately 8 million Americans purchased occult books, magazines, charms, voodoo pendants and other paraphernalia. The *Handbook of Supernatural Powers* has sold 529,521 copies and the *Magic Power of Witchcraft*, 121,365. The Air Force is considering admitting satanists to the chaplaincy, according to a report from Jim Ammerman of the Chaplaincy of Full Gospel Churches.

Mass killer Charles Manson appeared at his latest parole hearing with a satanist swastika painted on his forehead. Night stalker Richard Ramirez displayed the satanist pentagram painted on the palm of his hand and shouted, "Hail Satan," at his first court appearance. Some heavy metal rock music contains blatantly explicit satanist lyrics, and more subtle backward masking has been found on other rock records. Law enforcement officers are attending seminars instructing them how to detect and deal with ritualistic sexual child abuse and human sacrifice.

Many will quickly affirm, "None of my friends or relatives are into that kind of thing." That may be true, but I think Michael Harper displays a great deal of wisdom when he says, "It is my conviction that many people are prisoners of these evil powers and that they affect our lives physically, emotionally and spiritually far more than most people are prepared to admit."[13] Not that we're "looking for a demon behind every bush," as some say. But let's be clear. If there's a demon behind my bush, I want to get rid of it. And I believe you do, too.

Demons and Christians

When someone like Michael Harper makes a statement about the pervasive influence of demons in the world today, is he excluding Christians? Most Christians, myself included, wish it were true that demons could not harm Christians. Some have even formulated such wishes into doctrinal positions. One of the biggest surprises I received soon after I began to move in the third wave was what could be called the doctrine of Christian exemption from demonization.

I would not have been that surprised to hear such speculation from my own circle of evangelicals, where the level of understanding of and expertise in spiritual warfare was minor league at best. But the surprise came when I found that large numbers of Pentecostals agreed with traditional evangelicals on that point. In fact, some time ago the largest Pentecostal denomination of them all, the Assemblies of God, produced a 15-page official statement on "Can Born-Again Believers Be Demon Possessed?" Their answer was no. After working through biblical and historical arguments, the statement concludes, "It is a subtle trick of the devil that makes sincere people accuse Christians today of having a demon." The statement does not deny that demons are real and that some people are demonized, but it holds that the very fact that a person is demonized constitutes proof that he or she could not be a true Christian. "Only if we are cut off from the vine and cast forth as a dead branch can Satan or his demons claim us," it affirms.[14]

If I felt this were a matter of secondary importance, such as whether a church baptizes by sprinkling or whether real wine is served at communion or whether Jesus is coming before or after the tribulation, I wouldn't bring it up. But in my opinion it is a primary issue in ministry. When Jesus announced the agenda of the kingdom in the synagogue in Nazareth, one of His agenda items was to "set at liberty those who are oppressed" (Luke 4:18). If Christians are among the oppressed, they should be liberated. I believe that some are.

THE FULLER HASSLE

The hassle I found myself in at Fuller Seminary, which I

mentioned at the beginning of the chapter, revolved around this question. Many of my colleagues, I rapidly discovered, agreed with the Assemblies of God. One thing I learned through it all was that I needed to do more homework on the issue. And I have. The net result is that I still think born-again Christians can be demonized. Could I be wrong? Yes. I will be the first to admit

While the devil was defeated on the cross, he is not yet off the scene in the lake of fire, and meanwhile he is a formidable enemy.

that I am nervous matching my opinion against the Assemblies of God. Many of my friends whom I respect disagree with me, and they may be the ones who are right. How so?

As we have seen previously, the devil was defeated when Jesus went to the cross. The Holy Spirit, not the devil, dwells in every one of us who is a believer. Paul writes, "Do you not know that your body is the temple of the Holy Spirit who is in you, whom you have from God, and you are not your own?" (1 Cor. 6:19). As a result we can affirm with a great deal of faith that "He who is in you is greater than he who is in the world" (1 John 4:4). Put that all together, and you can make a good case for concluding that it is not possible for Satan or his demons to afflict a Christian.

But even those who make that argument don't usually carry it to an extreme. For example, they recognize Satan's active role in tempting even Christians to sin. Some temptation comes from the world and some comes from the flesh, but some also comes from the devil. They know that Peter was writing to Christians when he warned them to resist the devil, who is like a roaring lion. They seek daily to take up the shield of faith "with which you will be able to quench all the fiery darts of the wicked one" (Eph. 6:16). They know that, while the devil was defeated on the cross, he is not yet off the scene in the lake of fire, and meanwhile he is a formidable enemy. Some, including the Assemblies of God, will say that while Christians cannot be *possessed*, they can be *oppressed* by demons. With all this, maybe we're not so far apart in our opinions after all.

In my research, I have noticed several things. For one, almost all those who themselves are actively involved in a ministry of exorcism or deliverance affirm that Christians can be demonized. For another, I have discovered that several Christian leaders have changed their opinion on this matter in recent years. But the changes I have observed have all been in the same direction, namely, from once denying that demons can harm Christians to now affirming that they can and do.

For example, well-known pastor and author Charles Swindoll addresses the question of whether Christians can be demonized by saying, "For a number of years, I questioned this, but I am now convinced that it can occur." In his counseling ministry with Christians, Swindoll says, "On a few occasions I have assisted in the painful process of relieving them of demons."[15] Southern Baptist evangelist James Robison also says that there was a time when he did not believe that Christians needed deliverance ministry, until *he* was delivered from a demon that felt to him like a claw on his brain.[16] Edward Murphy of Overseas Crusades testifies he thought Christians were automatically protected from demonization, until his missionary experience in Latin

America and his counseling ministry with Christian students at Biola University forced him to reexamine his position.[17]

FRED DICKASON'S VIEWPOINT

I could quote others, such as Paul Yonggi Cho, Michael Green, Kurt Koch, Francis MacNutt, Jack Hayford, John Wimber, David du Plessis, Charles Kraft, Derek Prince or any number of other prominent Christian figures who have learned by experience that Christians can be demonized. But the strongest case I have yet seen supporting the idea that Christians can be demonized comes not from a Pentecostal or a charismatic but from a traditional evangelical, C. Fred Dickason. Dickason is chairperson of the Department of Theology in Moody Bible Institute. His book *Demon Possession and the Christian* contains 350 pages of carefully detailed reasoning.

Dickason first looks at biblical evidence. He painstakingly examines the biblical texts that have been used through the years to show that Christians cannot be demonized. Then he does the same with the texts that have been used on the other side of the argument. His conclusion: Neither side wins. The fact of the matter, according to Dickason, is that we can find no clear-cut biblical evidence either for or against the demonization of believers.

He goes on to do the same with the theological arguments and comes to the same conclusion. He says, "From the survey and analysis for arguments pro and con, we conclude that we cannot say with reasonable certainty that either position is correct."[18]

Dickason's next step is to turn to clinical evidence.

As he does, he uses a highly illuminating analogy. He proposes that before we go to the question as to whether Christians can be demonized, it would be helpful first to raise the question, Can Christians get cancer?

What does the Bible have to say about it? Well, the Bible says that disease is real, that it began to plague the human race as a result of sin, and that Christians and non-Christians alike can get sick. But there is no passage in the Bible that addresses the issue of whether Christians can get cancer.

In that case, we are justified in turning to human experience and looking at clinical evidence. This is not to place human experience on a level equal to or above divine revelation. When the Bible gives us clear teaching on a certain issue, we then interpret human experience in the light of revelation. But when the Bible is neutral on an issue, it is legitimate for us to learn and apply what we learn from human experience, so long as our conclusions don't contradict Scripture.

Clinical evidence shows that many people who profess to be born again, who are good church members, and who are considered Christians by others do, in fact, get cancer. So where does this leave us? If we have decided ahead of time that Christians can't get cancer, obviously no one who gets it could be a Christian, regardless of what he or she thinks. Such reasoning is obviously ridiculous. Just because the Bible doesn't say directly that Christians can get cancer is not enough evidence to reject reality.

But, Fred Dickason points out similar reasoning has been used to argue that Christians cannot be demonized. True, the Bible does not say directly that they can (although some texts strongly lean in that direction). But clinical evidence does show that people who by common consensus exhibit the marks of a true Christian have been and are today demonized.

As a starter, Dickason cites his own ministry. He says, "I have encountered from 1974 to 1987 at least 400 cases of those who were genuine Christians who were also demonized." While he concedes he is not infallible, he asserts, "I know the marks of a Christian and the marks of a demonized person."[19] In numerous cases his own diagnoses have been confirmed by pastors, psychologists and psychiatrists. He provides many concrete examples that add to the value of his excellent book.

Before I go on, I realize some will be saying, "Well, Wagner didn't prove biblically that Christians can be demonized." In one way that is correct, but in another it is not. While there is no passage of Scripture that deals directly with the issue, some important indirect references cannot be overlooked. When Paul, in Ephesians 6, tells us that we wrestle not against flesh and blood, but against principalities and powers and spiritual hosts of wickedness in the heavenly places, we must realize that he is writing to Christians. He says that we must take up the full armor of God (see Eph. 6:13) and that the wicked one shoots fiery darts at us (see Eph. 6:16). In other words, demons are real and Christians need to take special precautions to protect themselves. If they don't, they can be harmed. It's difficult to understand the passage otherwise.

Similarly, Peter warns fellow Christians to be sober and vigilant because "the devil walks about like a roaring lion, seeking whom he may devour" (1 Pet. 5:8). I mentioned this before, but I feel I should repeat it. Theologically speaking, the devil is not omnipresent—only God is. The devil does not do his evil work personally, but delegates it to multitudes of demons. So, when Peter goes on to tell Christians that we should resist the devil (see 1 Pet. 5:9), a reasonable conclusion would be that he is telling us to resist demons. Why would the Bible stress this if Christians could not be harmed by demons?

I am not saying this to frighten Christians—I am saying it to alert them. Speaking of Satan, Martin Luther said in "A Mighty Fortress" that "one little word shall fell him." That word is Jesus; and Jesus' power, mediated through the Holy Spirit, is more than any demon can match.

TERRITORIAL SPIRITS

Knowing that Christians can be demonized and that God gives us the power and authority to deliver them from oppression will help greatly when we seek to apply insights coming from the third wave to our own churches. But how about the outward focus of our ministry? How about evangelizing the lost? How about moving into the world to reach unreached people groups for Jesus Christ? Can the third wave help us here?

I believe it can in many ways. All I have said about power evangelism comes into play here. We have seen that signs and wonders are helping to bring large numbers of people into God's kingdom around the world. In many places a key to the spread of the gospel is the power encounter. But there is a subcategory of power encounter that has great potential for accelerating world evangelization and about which Christian leaders seem to know relatively little. I refer to breaking the power of territorial spirits.

We read in 2 Corinthians 4:4 that Satan has successfully blinded the minds of unbelievers so that they cannot receive the gospel. This undoubtedly refers to individuals, but could it also refer to territories? Could it mean nations? States? Cities? Cultural groups? Tribes? Social networks? In the parable of the sower, Jesus said that the seed of the Word falling on the road produces no fruit, because "Satan comes immediately and takes away the word that was sown in their hearts" (Mark 4:15). Church growth theory has long ago recognized the phenomenon of resistant peoples. Could it be that at least some of that resistance may be caused by the direct working of demonic forces?

Sumrall's Greatest Battle

To illustrate let's look at a dramatic event that occurred a number of years ago in the Philippines under the ministry of Lester Sumrall. He reports that he went on an extended evangelistic mission to the Philippines, because he felt he heard a direct word from God telling him to go and that great things would happen. But after five months of preaching, only five people were saved. Obviously, something was wrong.

One night Sumrall heard a radio report mention an inmate in the Bilibid Prison named Clarita Villanueva. Some unseen creature apparently was biting her, leaving deep teeth marks on her neck, arms and legs. She frequently behaved like an animal, biting, scratching and kicking the doctors. The media featured her case. During the radio broadcast Sumrall felt God calling him to go to the prison and cast demons out of her. He prayed all that night, and the next day asked permission from the mayor. The mayor said that she was a witch and that no one was allowed near her. But after Sumrall had signed a legal release, he was permitted to go to her cell.

The moment he saw her, one of the demons spoke in English (although the woman herself could not speak English); "I don't like you!" It cursed Sumrall, God and the blood of Christ. Sumrall says, "I went into the greatest battle of my life," but through the power of the Holy Spirit he got rid of the demons and led her to Christ. Sumrall reports that "150,000 people experienced salvation because of this great miracle" and "From that day the Philippines has had revival."[20]

I am not sure that we know for a fact whether the power of one or more territorial spirits was broken at that time. But in recent years the rate of church growth has greatly accelerated in the Philippines. I cite this event because I believe it is a type of ministry that we should take more seriously than many of us have in the past. I should think that, using Clarita Villanueva's deliverance as a hypothesis that some cosmic changes may have taken place, would be a potentially fruitful avenue of research for evangelism and church growth.

Argentine Spirits

Among my personal circle of friends, the one who has had the most experience in dealing with territorial spirits is Argentine Omar Cabrera, pastor of the Vision of the Future Church. A unique feature of his church is that it is decentralized, meeting in 40 or more cities simultaneously throughout the central region of Argentina. Omar and his wife, Marfa, travel 7,000 miles a month, mostly by automobile, leading the church, which numbers some 145,000. How does he move into a new location for his church?

His general practice, after the potential site is selected, is to check into a hotel and seclude himself alone in a room in prayer and fasting. It usually takes the first two or three days to allow the Holy Spirit to cleanse him, to help him disassociate from himself, and to identify with Jesus. He feels he "leaves the world" and is in another realm where the spiritual warfare takes place. The attacks of the enemy at times become fierce. He has even seen some spirits in physical form. His objective is to learn their names and break their power over the city. It usually takes five to eight days, but sometimes more. Once he spent 45 days in conflict. But when he finishes, people in his meetings frequently are saved and healed even before he preaches or prays for them.

Back in chapter 3 I described the tremendous growth of churches in Argentina today and the power evangelism that is accompanying it. I have talked for hours with friends like Omar Cabrera and Edgardo Silvoso listening to them analyze what seems to be behind the extraordinary moving of God in that nation since the Falkland Islands war of 1982. One hypothesis relates directly to the type of cosmic struggles I am describing here.

Back in the days when Juan Peron ruled the country, he used as his chief advisor a male witch, Jose Lopez Rega, who was a high priest of the Macumba strain of spiritism. Silvoso reports that Lopez Rega was the *de facto* power of the government, infiltrating the media, the business world and the military. A wave of demonic activity swept the country. People were giving testimonies on national television as to how they were helped by Macumba. Unfortunately, the evangelical community was ill-equipped to deal with all of this. As Silvoso told me, "We had sound doctrine, but we were powerless to combat demonic forces." Churches had not grown significantly in decades.

It is rumored that when Lopez Rega left the government, he placed a curse on Argentina that resulted in the inhuman atrocities under the rule of the military from 1976 to 1981. Civil rights were unknown. Thousands of people simply disappeared, now known to be raped, tortured, brutally murdered and thrown into secret mass graves, or dumped into the river. Then the change came in 1982. What exactly happened in the cosmic realm in 1982 we do not yet know. But, more than in any other place I know, the most prominent Christian leaders in Argentina, such as Omar Cabrera, Carlos Annacondia, Hector Gimenez and others, overtly challenge and curse Satan and his demonic forces both in private prayer and on public platforms. The nation as a whole apparently is engaged in a world-class power encounter.

Spirits in Other Lands

When I first met Omar Cabrera several years ago, I wondered if his ministry of breaking the power of territorial spirits was unique or whether others might know something about it as well. Since then my research has uncovered several reports from different parts of the world that seem to confirm the reality of what we are talking about. For example, Timothy Warner of Trinity Evangelical Divinity School believes that pioneer missionaries especially need to be prepared to break the power of spirits that rule territories. He relates incidents from missionaries to Indians in Canada and Papua New Guinea where this was actually done.[21]

Paul Yonggi Cho describes an interview with an

American Presbyterian chaplain who had experienced a dry, fruitless ministry among the military in Germany, but in Korea "suddenly heaven opens and the Spirit pours out." Cho says that in Germany "the powers of the sky were not broken because the German church did not pray." In Korea the "atmosphere of the air" is different, because the cosmic evil powers have been broken. In Korea, Cho says, "There is not so much pollution as we are a praying church." He cites the early morning prayer meetings, the all-night prayer meetings and the prayer mountains that are all very much a part of Korean church life.[22]

Jack M. Chisholm, pastor of the Glendale, California, Presbyterian Church, made an investigative trip to Korea. Among many lessons for growth and renewal he learned was his newfound conviction that we need to be able to "tackle the strongholds, to break down the towers, and to set people free." He believes that the new wave of the power of the Holy Spirit that many of us are seeing "will break the backs of demonic institutions that hold nations as well as people in bondage."[23]

Bill Jackson tells in *World Christian* magazine of a missionary couple in Thailand, who saw no fruit for years until they decided to set one day a week aside to go into the woods and engage the territorial spirits in warfare. A wave of conversions followed. Jackson believes that thousands of unreached peoples are currently under the direct thumb of Satan, and "The gospel won't go forward among these peoples until we bind the spirits that bind them, whether those deceptive forces be Islam, Hinduism, or any of a myriad of others."[24]

In recent years churches have been growing rapidly in Brazil, but very slowly in neighboring Uruguay. A missionary who met Ralph Mahoney of World MAP had a strange experience while distributing tracts in a small town on the border of Brazil and Uruguay, where the main street divided the two nations. He found that on the Uruguay side no one would accept the tracts, while they received them gratefully on the Brazilian side of the street. And individuals who refused them on the Uruguay side would change their attitude and take them on the Brazilian side. The missionary's interpretation was that "in crossing the street they were passing out from under the covering of darkness in Uruguay into a country that had experienced, in part, the removing of the covering."[25]

WHAT ARE THEIR NAMES?

Mark I. Bubeck sees Satan as the commander-in-chief of the forces of darkness, leading a hierarchical structure of evil spirits. The most powerful are *principalities* or *princes*. Bubeck understands them to have vast power and a certain degree of independence of action. Under them are *powers* "probably more numerous and somewhat less independent and powerful than the princes." Next are the *rulers of darkness* who serve as lower grade officers. Finally come the *wicked spirits* or *demons*.[26]

How territorial assignments are distributed throughout the hierarchy is unclear at this point. Perhaps further research will provide some answers. My colleague Charles Kraft has worked with Costa Rican psychologist Rita Cabezas de Krumm, who has carried on an extensive ministry of deliverance for some time. Reports that Kraft has secured from her provide the most extensive clues I have yet seen to the identity of top-ranked spirits.

In a two-hour struggle with a demon named Asmodeo, the demon identified himself as one of six princes that serve just under Satan, whom they regard as king. Each one of the six, he said, has charge of a certain type of work, Asmodeo himself assigned to vice, drugs, homosexuality, adultery, marriage destruction and overeating. In different places the same six princes may assume different names, but the others can be identified as Damian, Beelzebub, Nosferasteus, Arios and Menguelesh. Since demons are liars, one does not know exactly how much credence to give to such information, but I believe it is worth a continuing investigation as Rita Cabezas herself is carrying out.

Paul Lehmann, a missionary to Zaire with Christian and Missionary Alliance, recently published a list of the names of demons he cast out of a witch doctor, Tata Pembele. They included Guard of the Ancestors, Spirit of Travel, Feeder of the Dead, Rescuer from Sorcery, Voice of the Dead, Spreader of Illness, Paralyzer, Destroyer in Water, Healer and many others. Through them the witch doctor had exercised great power.[27]

Witches in the Los Angeles area chant to Isis, Astarte, Hecate, Demeter, Kali and Innana. Others bow to Cerridwen, Mother of Earth and Cernunnos, Father of the Woodlands. Paul Kauffman has identified a chief spirit of Thailand as Narai. Indians in the Andes acknowledge the power of Pachamama, Inti and Viracocha. Some Mexicans feel that the Aztec war god Huitzilopochtil still exercises power.

The names of two territorial spirits are apparently mentioned in Daniel 10. He speaks of an angel of God who was coming to minister to him, but who was delayed because of spiritual warfare with "the prince of the kingdom of Persia" (v. 13; see also v. 20) and who later expected a similar battle with the "prince of Greece" (v. 20). Paul refers to them as principalities and powers and "spiritual hosts of wickedness in the heavenly places" (Eph. 6:12).

THE SPIRIT OF MERIGILDO

Edgardo Silvoso was the speaker at one of our recent prayer retreats held at Lake Avenue Congregational Church in Pasadena, California. One of his topics was spiritual warfare. He told how in 1985 he and some friends had taken a map, drawn a circle with a 100-mile radius around his Harvest Evangelism leadership training center near Rosario, Argentina, and discovered that there were 109 towns within the circle with no evangelical church. They then found that in a town called Arroyo Seco a warlock named Merigildo had long exercised great power. He had trained 12 disciples, and when he died, he transferred his power to a spring of water. Once this was discovered, Christian leaders of the area, Pentecostal and non-Pentecostal, gathered together for a prayer meeting to do spiritual warfare. Silvoso reports that it was the most powerful prayer meeting he had ever attended. They took dominion over the area in the name of Jesus.

Six of them then went to the headquarters of Merigildo in Arroyo Seco, Silvoso among them. They served public notice that he was defeated by the blood of Christ, pointed their car toward the headquarters building, and broke the evil power in the name of Jesus.

The results? In less than three years after Merigildo's power was broken, 82 of the 109 towns had an evangelical church, and more were rapidly being planted.

There is much more to learn about resisting the devil. We have many questions and not enough answers. But one answer that we do have is that Jesus is building His Church, and the power of the Holy Spirit is more than sufficient so that "the gates of Hades shall not prevail against it" (Matt. 16:18).

Notes _____

1. Francis MacNutt, *Healing* (Notre Dame, IN: Ave Maria Press, 1974), p. 208.
2. Michael Green, *I Believe in Satan's Downfall* (Grand Rapids, MI: Wm. B. Eerdmans Pub. Co., 1981), p. 10.
3. John Wimber, "The Reality of Spiritual Warfare," *First Fruits*, Nov. 1984, p. 3.
4. H. Newton Malony, "Diseased, Deluded, Depraved, Demonized: Options in diagnosis for religious mental health professionals," paper presented at the annual meeting of the American Academy of Religion, Anaheim, CA, Nov. 1985, p. 135.
5. Ibid.
6. Colin Brown, editor, *The New International Dictionary of New Testament Theology* (Grand Rapids, MI: Zondervan Publishing House, 1975), Vol. 1, p. 453.
7. John Wimber with Kevin Springer, *Power Healing* (San Francisco: Harper and Row, 1987), p. 109.
8. Valdemar Kroker, "Spiritism in Brazil," *Mission Focus*, Mar. 1987, p. 1.
9. Ibid., p. 5.
10. John Maust, "The Land Where Spirits Thrive," *Christianity Today*, Dec. 13, 1985, p. 50.
11. Kroker, "Spiritism in Brazil," p. 1.
12. Maust, "The Land," p. 50.
13. Michael Harper, *Spiritual Warfare* (Downers Grove, IL: InterVarsity Press, 1986), p. 33.
14. General Presbytery of the Assemblies of God, "Can Born-Again Believers Be Demon Possessed?" Springfield, MO, May 1972, p. 15.
15. Charles R. Swindoll, *Demonism* (Portland, OR: Multnomah Press, 1981), pp. 18,19.
16. James Robison, "Set Free From Thoughts That Destroy," *People of Destiny*, Mar./Apr. 1986, pp. 12-15.
17. Edward Murphy, "What Is the Devil Doing to Believers?" *Christian Life*, Feb. 1983, pp. 52-55.
18. C. Fred Dickason, *Demon Possession and the Christian*, (Chicago: Moody Press, 1987), p. 147.

19. Ibid., p. 175.
20. Lester Sumrall, "Deliverance: Setting the Captives Free," *World Harvest*, July/Aug. 1986, p. 7.
21. Timothy M. Warner, "Power Encounter with the Demonic," *Evangelism on the Cutting Edge*, Robert E. Coleman, ed. (Old Tappan, NJ: Fleming H. Revell Co., 1986), pp. 98,99.
22. Paul Yonggi Cho and C. Peter Wagner, eds., *Church Growth Manual No. 1*, Seoul: Church Growth International, 1986, p. 41.
23. Jack M. Chisholm, "Go to Korea and Learn From Them," *The Forerunner*, June 1984, p. 23.
24. Bill Jackson, "Waging War," *World Christian*, Jan./Feb. 1985, p. 11.
25. Ralph Mahoney, "The Covering of Darkness," *World MAP Digest*, Mar./Apr. 1983, p. 3.
26. Mark I. Bubeck, *The Adversary* (Chicago: Moody Press, 1975), pp. 72,73.
27. Paul Lehmann, "Invading Satan's Territory," *The Alliance Witness*, Mar. 18, 1987, p. 19.

NINE

DOING IT IN YOUR CHURCH

T he proof of the third wave is in the doing. Faith is necessary, but faith without works is dead. I have spent most of my time so far in this book attempting to build faith. We have seen that the third wave is real, that power evangelism is making a tre-mendous impact throughout today's world, that signs and wonders are part of the life-style of the kingdom of God, that Jesus passed His power to His followers, including us, and that part of serving God is to be engaged in spiritual warfare.

The question now is: Can all this happen in your church through your life and your ministry? I believe the answer is yes.

As I mentioned previously, my dream is that by the end of the century, overt up-front ministries of praying for the sick will be as common in churches across the board as Sunday School is now. It will be because, unless I miss my guess, this is one of the major things the Father is doing today. Hundreds of thousands of Pentecostal and charismatic churches have been praying for the sick in their churches for decades now. Many third-wave churches are also becoming involved. But, at least here in the U.S., the vast majority of churches have not yet incorporated divine healing into their philosophies of ministry. This chapter is principally directed to those churches.

The phrase, "how to have a healing ministry without making your church sick," is intriguing. Many chuckle when they first hear it because it touches, in a somewhat oblique way, one of the major problem areas of some models of healing we have all seen, namely, that they have tended to be divisive. Who does not have stories, either firsthand or secondhand, about healing ministries that split local churches, caused havoc in denominational annual meetings, upset parachurch organizations and produced long-standing personal enmities between Christian brothers and sisters on all levels? As a result, many churches have decided, on that basis, that they are simply not going to subject themselves to the hassle of advocating divine healing. And their negative image will not be changed unless they somehow perceive that it can be done with positive, rather than negative, effects on their congregation.

One of the objectives of the third wave is to help change these negative attitudes.

WHY PRAY FOR THE SICK?

One of Robert Schuller's slogans that has become part

of the mental furniture of Christian leaders across the nation is, "The secret of success is to find a need and fill it." It has caught on because it is so true.

Good health is the number one concern of most human beings. General observation itself would tell us that. One look at the annual cash flow of health care specialists would confirm it. When we list the professions of the wealthy, doctors and psychologists and dentists are automatically included. Furthermore, a recent scientific survey by the Gallup Poll and its affiliated organizations in other nations has given us statistical reinforcement. They found that in six nations of the world, health ranked first in importance among human concerns, with family running a close second.[1]

Churches have already known this, if you think about it. Check out the list of public prayer requests shared with congregations during any given week. Whether the requests are shared verbally at a Wednesday night prayer meeting, printed on special prayer request sheets, listed in the Sunday bulletin or announced from the pulpit, 70 to 90 percent are concerned with health. Praying for the sick is already a part of the ministry of every church I know. What is the problem then? The problem is that not many sick people who are prayed for are perceived to be healed as a direct result of the prayers. The power released through praying for the sick in most churches leaves a great deal to be desired. Here is where I hope we can see some measurable improvement in the days to come.

Many people are not as opposed to divine healing as we may think. Of course, as we have seen, belief in supernatural healing is widespread among cultures of the Third World. But even here in our technological culture of the United States, many are open to God's miraculous work. A recent Gallup survey in Orange County, California, found that no fewer than 47 percent of residents there believe in faith healing through miracles. And Orange County is not a hotbed of Christianity, with only 27 percent born again as compared to 40 percent nationwide, and with some of the lowest national figures on church membership and attendance.[2]

> *Few undertakings in life are win-win situations, but praying for the sick is one.*

So what does this mean? It means that most Americans are vitally concerned about their health, and around half already believe that God can heal them. Churches exist to bring people into contact with God and His power. So if churches are really concerned about people and their needs, as they say they are, what would stop them from adding healing the sick to their list of ministries? Not that healing the sick is the most important item on God's agenda—finding the lost and bringing them to eternal salvation is. But, still, when many people see that churches love them enough to be concerned about their immediate needs, hearts then open to consider the deeper and more eternal issues like salvation.

NOTHING TO LOSE

Few undertakings in life are win-win situations, but praying for the sick is one. I don't mean there are never any breakdowns or bad trips, but at least in my experience they are exceedingly rare. For example, last year I prayed one-on-one for perhaps 200 individuals, and so far as I can remember, every one had a positive experience. Not that all were healed, as I will explain in the next chapter, but all were ministered to. I like what Charles Kraft frequently says, "The issue is not healing but ministry."

To illustrate, I taught a two-week intensive course in church growth not too long ago and began each day with a prayer time as usual. One of my students named Dave, a church consultant, said that he had suffered from severe allergies for three years and was taking a shot every day to help control them. Would we pray? Another of the students was Pastor Che Ahn of the Abundant Life Community Church in Pasadena, California. Ahn spoke up and gave a testimony of how he had been miraculously healed of allergies. As he testified, I felt that God was saying that Ahn should go over to lay hands on Dave and see if God would give a special word as to how to pray. As Ahn approached him, he perceived in the Spirit that the man was under an evil curse, which he broke in the name of Jesus.

On Wednesday, Dave spoke up in the prayer time and said, "For three days now I have had no allergy symptoms. But even more important to me, this experience has bonded me to God in a way that I have never felt before. Even if the symptoms come back, my new relationship to God will not change." He later said that he had gone off all medication and that there were still no symptoms, adding that "only those who have suffered from allergies will be able to understand the meaning of what I am saying."

In this case, we won on both counts. But suppose the symptoms had come back, and they may have since then, for all I know. We still would have won, because the concern of the whole class, the love that was shown, the desire to minister to Dave's needs and the touch of the Holy Spirit in his inner person combined to produce a life-changing experience.

WHO CAN PRAY FOR THE SICK?

As I pointed out in the first chapter, one of the characteristics of the third wave is that the entrance point is through ministry rather than through a dramatic spiritual experience usually called baptism in the Holy Spirit. I also mentioned that the outworking of that ministry involves participating in what God is doing through the whole Body of Christ, rather than stressing individualistic performance. Many people take strong exception to the type of ministry they observe in some of our television faith healers. There the focus too often is on the individual healer rather than on the Body of Christ. I am not saying that God cannot or does not work in both ways. I am simply describing the style of the third wave as I understand it.

To come to the point, I believe that every Christian person should be active in a ministry of laying hands on the sick and praying for their recovery. I do not think that this should be restricted to clergy, elders or other church leaders or even to those with the gift of healing. I agree with Pastor Robert Wise, who says that "a healing ministry is available to the whole church, not just to some unique or elite group within it. There is a place for everyone to exercise this ministry who cares enough to pray for others."[3]

In my 120 Fellowship Sunday School class, for example, we have several who are recognized as having the spiritual gift of healing, but we encourage all to pray for the sick, whether they have the gift or not. God brings some individuals to the class who have heard by word of mouth that we minister to the sick and who need special help. One of these was Pamela Reddy, who had been told by doctors that she needed her diseased right kidney removed. She was recovering from hepatitis, she had been exposed to tuberculosis at the hospital where she worked, and due to an injury to her shoulder and neck her left arm did not function well or without pain (she is left-handed). Doctors had told her she would never have full use of her arm or freedom from pain.

After class she found her way to the church prayer chapel, where our class prayer team ministers for one hour each Sunday morning. There she was greeted by George and Pam Marhad, who pray for the sick on a regular basis, but who are not known to have received special gifts of healing. They laid on hands and prayed. The pain in Pamela Reddy's kidney disappeared, and her shoulder gained mobility. Over the next few weeks other prayers were answered, and she found a new place to live and a new job. When she underwent a physical examination for her new job, all her tests came back negative. There was no kidney disease and no residue of hepatitis or TB. Her neck had straightened, the bones in her shoulder were no longer rubbing and she had full range of motion in her arm, with no pain.[4]

When God works with healing power, He does not require superstars as His agents. He can and does work through ordinary, obedient Christians who understand and live the life-style of the kingdom of God. One of the most dramatic healings I have seen recently was that of missionary Sam Sasser, mentioned in chapter 4, who was lame and blind from coral poisoning. The person whose prayer God used was that of David Ellis, who had never had a healing ministry or even been involved in a group like the 120 Fellowship.

GIFTS AND ROLES

How do we understand this biblically? In my book *Your Spiritual Gifts Can Help Your Church Grow*, I identify and define 27 spiritual gifts that I feel God distributes throughout the Body of Christ. These are special attributes for ministry, which God gives by His grace to every member of the Body of Christ. I happen to believe that every Christian has one and usually more than one of these gifts, which God expects them to use for His glory. But I also believe that every Christian has a role to minister in almost every area of gifting, whether they have the specific gift or not. For instance, God has given a gift of faith to certain individuals, but every believer has a role of living a life of faith. Some have the gift of evangelist, but every Christian has a role of being a witness. Those with the gift of hospitality may be better at it and do it more often, but every Christian has a role to be hospitable. The same could be said about the gift of teaching, the gift of mercy, the gift of giving, the gift of discernment of spirits and the others. It also applies to the gift of healing.

I have received a gift of healing, while George and Pam Marhad have not. They have other gifts that I don't have. Because I have the gift, I believe that God is holding me to a higher degree of responsibility and accountability in my stewardship of the gift than others who do not have it. But, as a Body we should all be prepared to pray for the sick, whether from a gift base or a role base.

I have no expectation whatsoever that had I prayed for Pamela Reddy God would have healed her any more quickly or more thoroughly than He did through the Marhads. In fact, I am sure that God chose the Marhads to do it instead of me, because Pamela had needs other than the physical healing that the Marhads were able to minister to much better than I. This, in my opinion, is the way the Body of Christ has been designed to operate.

I happen to have the gift of healing, but I do not have gifts of pastor, exhortation, mercy or service. Therefore, I have found that I am at my best praying for a healing once. If it is healed then, fine. But if more is required, such as what Francis MacNutt calls "soaking prayer" or inner healing or pastoral counseling, I have neither the ability nor the inclination to become involved. So I turn the person over to the class prayer team or the pastoral care team, which have members who are gifted in those areas and who do a fine job under the power of the Holy Spirit. I am grateful that God hasn't called me to do it all, but that He has made me a part of a Body that He controls.

Speaking of gifts, do not be surprised to find that some with the gift of healing have been given specialties in certain areas. Francis MacNutt, for example, has had little success in praying for deafness, but a fairly high degree of success in praying for bone problems and problems in the abdominal or chest area, except cancer.[5] My specialty, as I have mentioned, is for lengthening legs (which in most cases involves pelvic adjustments) and problems relating to the spine. Others are best at inner healing. This is not unusual. We expect that some with the gift of evangelist may specialize in personal evangelism, while others will specialize in public evangelism. Some with the gift of teaching may use it better with adults, others with children. Some are versatile enough to do it all.

While ideally every Christian should be praying for the sick, some resist it for one reason above most others. It is too much of a risk for them. Here is how Pastor John Gunstone tells of his early experience: "I had one great fear. What would be the effect on a sick person if I prayed for their healing but they felt no improvement?" He confesses he still feels the fear to a degree, but he regularly prays for the sick, because, first, he realizes that it is God who does the healing, not him; and second, "I cannot remember anyone becoming seriously embittered because the prayer for healing was not answered as we'd hoped."[6] The fears that some of us have that we could make God look bad do not seem to be shared by the Almighty. God can pretty well take care of Himself. He just wants us to obey.

WHEN AND WHERE DO WE PRAY FOR THE SICK?

Once we are committed to praying for the sick as a part of living the life-style of the kingdom, as I hope we all will be, when and where do we pray? Obviously we need to pray whenever and wherever we can. But because we are human and have our individual limitations, it often helps to systematize our ministry. It makes sense to me to think of exercising a ministry of praying for the sick on four levels:

1. We Pray in Our Family Circle.

It should become second nature to lay on hands and

pray for our spouses, our children and others who are in our home when sickness comes. By this I do not mean that we attempt to bypass the medical profession. But in all too many Christian homes the medicine cabinet, the doctor's office and the hospital are not only our first recourse when illness strikes but our only one. Why not both pray and go to the doctor? Sometimes God chooses to heal directly, and sometimes He chooses to use means for the healing such as injections and operations. But He seldom heals directly unless we ask Him to.

I rarely suffer from digestive problems of any kind. But some days ago, when I first started to write this book, I developed a stomach upset just before noon, and by evening I was sick. I went to bed early, expecting to be well in the morning, but I woke up still sick. I knew the stomach flu was going around, because several of my friends had been down with it for the better part of a week. I had a whole day of writing ahead of me, and I needed my full level of energy. So I called my wife over, I stretched out on the bed and said, "I need an official healing prayer." So Doris laid hands on, prayed against the sickness and, thank God, I had no further problem.

There are those who will ask why I mention such a trivial thing. In fact, a number of my friends have objected quite strenuously when I have told stories like this. Some feel that suffering has a redemptive value and that I would be a better Christian and closer to God if I put up with the stomachache rather than ask God to take it away. Others wonder why I should think God would be concerned about my stomach flu when we know that His real concern is "apartheid in South Africa" or "civil war in Nicaragua." All I can say is that I mention it here precisely because it is relatively trivial, and I feel that God is glorified even in the small things when family members display enough love for each other and enough faith in God to pray for healing. I can imagine how I would have felt if my wife, instead of laying on hands, would have said, "Don't worry about it, Sweetheart. It's just the flu, and you'll get over it like everyone else. Meanwhile, learn the lessons God is trying to teach you." Shades of Job's comforters!

2. We Pray in the Routine of Everyday Life.

We all live different lives and have varying routines. My office schedule is tight, but I try to make room in it when someone needs prayer for healing. It is usually a matter of only 5 or 10 minutes.

As I have mentioned previously, I use the first 20 to 30 minutes of each class session for prayer (my classes run from two to six hours each). At first, I wondered if my students would complain. There may be one or two in a given class who do, but one of the most frequent positive comments on my class evaluations has been how much the prayer times have meant to the students. I taught a doctoral level class in church growth for pastors in Australia recently, for example. God was good, and some very remarkable things happened in our prayer times. One day one of the pastors brought his teenage son, who had a hip injury that was keeping him from playing cricket, so we prayed for him with laying on of hands. Later Pastor Philip Woolford wrote:

> Another aspect of the course's blessing was the times of prayer. As the days progressed, I came asking myself, "What is the Spirit of

God going to do today?" Personally it was a faith-lifting experience to be in such a faith climate, and it certainly gave the six hours of teaching integrity and freshness. Just the other day I was talking to Ross Weymouth, and I asked him how his son was. He was the one who injured his hip while very young and has suffered greatly since that time. Ross said that the hip and the leg had remained healed and restored since that day. Honestly, you cannot remain the same after seeing such a miracle.

I also try to be sensitive to openings to pray for people when I am traveling or at conferences. In such cases it is important to sense what the Father is doing, to avoid seeming rude or presumptuous. Timing is crucial. I recall that during the international meeting of the Lausanne Committee for World Evangelization held in January 1987 in Callaway Gardens, Georgia, a severe flu totally disabled three of the top leaders, namely, Bishop Jack Dain, a past president; Don Hoke, the treasurer; and Thomas Wang, the newly elected international director.

I thought of praying for them, but somehow couldn't get the green light from God to do it. This seemed strange, because I knew that members of the 120 Fellowship were praying that God would use me for healing while I was there. Jack Dain had been in bed for two days when God led Thomas Zimmerman, former general superintendent of the Assemblies of God, to lay hands on him and pray. His fever dropped from 102 back to normal almost instantly, and later that day Jack was up and around. When Bishop Dain gave a public testimony of God's intervention, I felt a twinge of envy. *Why had God chosen Tom instead of me?* Don Hoke had a light case and quickly got well. But Thomas Wang was in bed Tuesday, Wednesday, Thursday and Friday with no improvement. The problem was complicated, because he was scheduled to make a crucially important trip to Europe that very Sunday.

I needed to check out early on Friday, and while I was alone at the hotel desk, Leighton Ford's wife, Jeannie, suddenly appeared and we started talking. Among other things she mentioned that Thomas Wang was worse and that he would have to cancel his trip to Europe on Sunday. As she was speaking, I realized that God was talking to me through her and showing me that the timing was now right. So before I left, I went to his room. His wife, Rachel, opened the door. It was dark, and he was totally covered up and asleep. But I knew what had to be done, so I woke him up. His eyes were bleary, and he could hardly talk. I anointed him with oil and prayed specifically that he could go to Europe on Sunday. When I finished, he sat up in bed, stretched and said, "I don't know if this is just my imagination, but I think I feel better." I left for the airport. A few days later a mutual friend hand delivered a note Thomas had written on Saturday: "Thank you for your prayer yesterday. By now all symptoms are gone, and I am leaving for Europe tomorrow. Praise the Lord. He is still working today as He did 2000 years ago."

I have had to establish some limitations as to what I can or cannot do. For example, I never make house calls or hospital calls to pray for the sick. I feel that I have neither time nor energy to extend myself that much. When the need arises, I call on members of my prayer team or pastoral care team for this type of ministry.

3. We Pray in Small Groups.

A very natural place to pray for the sick is in meetings of small groups. These can be Sunday School classes, home Bible study meetings, task-oriented groups or any other occasions in which Christians meet on a regular basis.

4. We Pray in the Whole Church.

There are many ways of introducing a healing ministry into the whole church, but I will mention only three here. As illustrations, I will cite three pastors, all personal friends of mine, who have successfully introduced third-wave type of healing ministries in their churches without making their churches sick.

The mildest of the three is my own pastor, Paul Cedar. Some time ago as he was preaching through the book of James, God especially impressed him with the passage in chapter 5 on praying for the sick. Simultaneously a deacon's wife who was seriously ill followed this teaching, called the church leaders, had them anoint her with oil and pray, and she was remarkably healed. From that time on, Paul Cedar organized a church prayer team (my wife is one of the members), who pray for the sick after each of the three Sunday services. At the end of each service, Pastor Cedar invites those who need prayer for healing and anything else to go out a certain door leading to the prayer room after the service is dismissed. There the prayer team ministers to them, and numerous cases of healing have been reported.[7]

A bolder step was taken not long ago by Lloyd Ogilvie, pastor of the Hollywood, California, Presbyterian Church. He ends each worship service with a public invitation for people to come forward for prayers by the elders, in the front of the sanctuary during the closing hymn, making prayer for healing an integral part of the service. Ogilvie says, "To make a healing ministry a part of Sunday morning worship is mainlining that emphasis into the lifeblood of the Body of Christ."[8]

Robert Wise, pastor of Our Lord's Community Church in Oklahoma City (a Reformed Church of America congregation), goes further in scheduling and publicly advertising some regular Sunday evening services as healing services. They call it The Fellowship of the Healing Christ and use a fairly structured liturgy as an order of service. The word is out around the community, and many people, even from other churches, come for prayer or bring sick friends and relatives to be healed.

WHO SHOULD WE PRAY FOR?

My policy is to pray for anyone who asks for it, believer or unbeliever, even though I might have some inkling ahead of time that not much will happen. John Wimber reports that the most difficult people to pray for are those associated with the Word of Faith Movement. Fundamental Pentecostals are next, then liberal charismatics, then non-Pentecostal evangelicals, then liberals, and the easiest for him are non-Christians. How much this spectrum can be generalized I do not yet know. I am most apprehensive in praying for people who travel to Pasadena just for me to pray for them, especially when they fly here. I suppose I have a lingering fear that they might waste their money. But God often works despite my lack of faith.

One of the visitors I was particularly nervous about

was Ruth Silvoso, who flew down from San Jose, California. I had been acquainted with Ruth for some time, but I was much closer to her husband, Edgardo Silvoso (whom I have mentioned several times) and her brother, Luis Palau. Ruth had been born with a short leg, which had been causing severe back pain for the past 10 years. She wrote later, "When Dr. Wagner and his wife, Doris, prayed for me, right there before our eyes my husband,

> *There is no secret formula, ritual or procedure, which, when used correctly, makes the healing happen. God does the healing, and we cannot write His script for Him.*

Ed, and I saw a healing miracle. My leg grew before us as we watched God work. I felt heat from my upper leg to my toe. I had the same sensation when he prayed for my back and neck. I used to have tension on my neck, pain in the upper back, and headaches. Now I have no pain at all. Praise the Lord!"

HOW DO WE PRAY FOR THE SICK?

There are many different approaches to praying for the sick. Up to this point I cannot identify any that are more or less effective. Oral Roberts, one of the most prominent faith healers, stresses a Point of Contact, "something tangible—something you DO . . . and when you DO IT, you release your faith toward God."[9] Omar Cabrera does not practice the laying on of hands but calls forth sick people and prays for them as a group. Carlos Annacondia touches people, and they fall backward "slain in the Spirit." Reinhard Bonkke has people in the crowd put their hand where it hurts and prays for them all.

I recall that I was doing four pastors' conferences on church growth in South Africa some time ago, teamed up with a black South African evangelist, Elijah Maswanganyi. I taught in the day, and he preached at night. The first night he asked if I would join him in praying for the sick, and I readily agreed. When he gave the invitation, about 50 people came forward for prayer. Elijah said, "You start on the left, and I'll start on the right." I used the approach that I will describe later, and the first woman I prayed for needed some extra attention. When I finished, I got up to go to the next person and found to my surprise that Elijah had prayed for all 49 others in the meantime. His approach was different from mine, and so far as I know, our rate of healing is about the same.

What I am saying is that there is no secret formula, ritual or procedure, which, when used correctly, makes the healing happen. God does the healing, and we cannot write His script for Him. The four Christian leaders I mentioned above have all been used remarkably as channels of God's healing for thousands of people. My suggestion is not to look for the right or the wrong way to pray for the sick, but to look for the way that best fits you and your particular philosophy of ministry.

WIMBER'S FIVE STEPS

The procedure for praying for the sick that seems to fit many third-wave churches revolves around John Wimber's five steps. The steps are easy, they can be learned quickly, they are very low key and they are as effective as anything else I have seen. I use Wimber's five steps, the 120 Fellowship prayer team uses them, I teach them in my classes at Fuller Seminary and I recommend them here. The five steps have been so widely disseminated that you may see slightly different steps in different people's lists. But I will explain them as John Wimber outlines them in his book *Power Healing*.[10]

Step 1: The Interview

Have the person sit in a chair and converse a little to relax them. The questions in the interview will vary, but the main purpose is to find out specifically what they want you to pray for. Ask where it hurts, how long they have had it, how and when it started, what others have said about it, what treatment they have received and other similar questions. Don't try to complete a medical history (that can be boring and distracting), but do find out where they are coming from. It is necessary to listen, not only to the sick person, but also to God, for sometimes God will reveal special information during the interview. You may feel you have a special hunch or get a similar impression.

This happened to me when I was praying for a cancer patient not long ago. A supporter of Fuller Seminary called my dean, Paul Pierson, and asked if he could arrange for me to pray for a friend of his. We set up a meeting at Pierson's home, and his friend was driven there by her daughter. In the interview she said she wanted to be healed from cancer that had been found in her liver, colon and other organs. But as I talked to her, God impressed upon me the thought: Pray for her salvation. So at that point I changed the whole procedure. She turned out to be a churchgoer who had never established a personal relationship with Jesus Christ as Savior and Lord. But God had totally prepared her to be saved, and I had the privilege of leading first her, then her daughter, to Christ. After that, I prayed against the cancer. Whether the cancer was healed, I do not yet know, but I do know that a much more important issue was settled, her eternal destiny.

Step 2: The Diagnostic Decision

While the interview is taking place, try to discern what is the underlying cause of the symptoms. Sometimes physical symptoms have their roots in emotional or spiritual problems. It might be that inner healing needs to precede physical healing. Those who have pastoral gifts or the gift of discerning of spirits find that they frequently use them at this point. It is also the time when some may receive a word of knowledge that helps them understand more precisely what is going on.

I have found that I do not have much insight when it comes to the diagnosis. I usually direct my attention to the symptoms described in the interview. I'm sure that at least some of those I pray for who are not healed would be healed if I were more skilled at diagnosis, but I'm not. Nevertheless, I do try to keep my spiritual antenna tuned to what God wants to say to me.

One day after one of my doctor of ministry classes a pastor asked me to pray for him. I discovered through the interview that for a month he had been suffering from acute pain between his shoulders and up his neck. This was one of the unusual times that God let me know specifically what the problem was, so I said, "Are you contemplating a change in your ministry?"

His eyes widened, and he gave me a puzzled look. "How did you know?" he asked.

It turned out that he was planning to leave his present parish, but it was still a carefully kept secret. I asked when he made his decision, and he said a month ago, as I had suspected. I told him that I would pray for his neck, but that I didn't believe the pain would go until he resolved some of the problems involved in his decision.

The next day the pain was still there. Then in the evening he had a long conversation with his roommate, who helped him work through some problems. His roommate then laid hands on him, prayed, and that was the end of his pain. The following day he expressed his delight to be free from pain for the first time in a month.

Step 3: The Prayer Selection

Once you know what you are going to pray for, you need to decide how you will pray. Sometimes it's almost impossible to know how God will choose to heal someone. In one of my classes we prayed for a South African pastor who had severe back pains. The next day he testified that after class he was filling his car with gasoline, slipped on some grease and fell hard on the cement. From that moment on he experienced no more pain. "It was a divine chiropractic adjustment," he quipped.

The most common type of prayer is *intercession*, in which you simply ask God specifically to heal whatever is wrong. Another is *command*, in which you speak directly to the body part, pain, swelling or tumor and tell it to leave or die or be dissolved, or whatever is necessary. If you feel an evil spirit may be involved, a prayer of *rebuke* may be in order.

At this point you also decide whether to use oil. I carry a vial of oil—which has been consecrated for healing—in my pocket at all times. Sometimes I anoint the person with it, sometimes I don't, depending on how I feel God is leading during the prayer selection phase. Some use holy water. Some use consecrated salt. Some use the sacrament of holy communion. Others use none of the above, but depend on prayer alone. So many people I respect do it so many different ways that I hesitate to recommend any one above the others. I find the oil is best for me.

Step 4: The Prayer Engagement

John Wimber has taught us to pray with our eyes open, and it seems to work very well. The major reason for this is that it allows us to see what, if anything, the Holy Spirit is doing in a physical way. Sometimes there is a trembling, a fluttering of eyelids or a kind of aura that surrounds the person. Sometimes there are other manifestations.

At a leadership conference I was doing, one of the persons attending came up after a session and urgently asked me to pray for him. He suffered from chronic asthma, and had experienced a strong attack during my session. At that point he could hardly breathe, and each breath caused sharp pain. By the time I got to Step 3 I had become strongly suspicious that it was a demonic attack, so my prayer choice was a command of deliverance. I commanded the spirit of asthma to leave immediately. The man coughed loudly, a puff of white smoke came out of his mouth and he could breathe freely from then on. I wouldn't have known what had happened had I closed my eyes during prayer.

I believe that an active prayer is more effective than a passive prayer. More timid souls, in order to cover their bases and create a fail-safe situation, will pray, "God, I don't know what your will is, but if it is your will, please heal this person." The basic principle is sound, namely, that we want nothing other than God's will to be done. But frequently this type of prayer reflects not only submission to God's will, which is good, but also lack of faith and lack of discernment, which are not. As we gain experience in listening to God as well as talking to Him, we will, in many cases, be able to know what His will is by the time we get through the first three steps. This enables us to pray with a degree of boldness that otherwise we could not have, and the active approach does seem to release more healing power than the passive approach. I think it is a more direct attack on Satan's kingdom. With the exception of the Garden of Gethsemane, we don't see Jesus using the passive approach.

Step 5: Post-prayer Direction

After the prayer ask the people how they feel. You'll want to know if anything happened. Assure them that they don't have to feel anything in order to receive healing, but sometimes they do. If the symptoms are gone, rejoice together and praise God. If the symptoms are still there, sometimes you will want to pray again immediately. Sometimes you will want to invite them to come back. You may suggest that this time God may be healing gradually, rather than instantaneously.

Sometimes I feel led to recommend that the person I have been praying for find another person or another group to pray more. When possible I refer them to my 120 Fellowship prayer team. In every case, I assure them of God's love and that God will be with them whether they are sick or well.

When the person is under medical treatment, I always advise them to check out the results with their physician. If they are currently taking medication, they should not stop taking it until the doctor who prescribed it advises them to stop. Many times I tell the person that I feel God is going to heal them through health professionals rather than directly, and I remind them that this is no less God at work. I agree with Jack Hayford, who says, "We should always be people who know the receiving of medical help is not a rejection of divine healing."[11]

Whatever the result of the prayer, keep the person honest. I see no value in pretending that symptoms are not there by "claiming it." I realize that some feel that admitting the symptoms are still there betrays a lack of faith and constitutes a blockage to healing, and I respect those who advocate that position, because God is using many of them in a remarkable way. But I have found the up-front, tell-it-like-it-is approach most helpful. And others have told me they appreciate it very much as well.

WORDS OF KNOWLEDGE

In connection with Step 2, the diagnosis, I mentioned that God may at times provide a word of knowledge for specific guidance. What is this word of knowledge, and how does it operate?

I personally believe that word of knowledge used in this context is a misnomer. I think the spiritual gift called knowledge as found in 1 Corinthians 12:8 is related to scholarship, as I explain in my book *Your Spiritual Gifts Can Help Your Church Grow.* I see the word of knowledge as it is currently used to be a sub-set within the broad gift of prophecy. But I have reluctantly joined those who use this term in the loose contemporary sense, because for one thing I find it takes me too long to explain what I think is the correct meaning, and for another this is an extremely minor point.

What we do agree on is that the so-called word of knowledge is a revelatory gift. That is, through the gift, God speaks to people, as He does in other forms of prophecy as well. I realize that some will raise theological red flags at this point and argue that God's revelation ceased with the closing of the canon of Scripture. I am not going to pause to argue against that point of view at this time, except to say I do think the position can be shown to be untenable. I believe God continually desires to reveal His words to us, although not on the level that we find enscripturated in the Bible. Furthermore, any revelation through word of knowledge or other prophecy must always be tested for validity against Scripture.

What Are They For?

Words of knowledge help us greatly in praying for the sick, because they allow us to understand more specifically just what the Father is doing. And once we know what He is doing, we can then act with greater boldness and faith.

For example, Floyd McClung, Director of International Operations for Youth With A Mission (YWAM), once told me about his wife, Sally's, first missionary experience. She was 16 at the time, on a team of eight teenagers in the Samoan Islands. The senior missionary supervising them took out a map and indicated several villages they could evangelize. But, pointing his finger, he said, "No matter what you do, don't go to this one. We have tried. The chief is hostile and has declared his village a closed village. He has surrounded the village with several packs of wild dogs to keep strangers out."

When the teenagers prayed, they received a word of knowledge in which God told them to go to that particular village. They had all the normal human fears and misgivings, but they decided to obey. They approached the village. The dogs charged. But when they got near to the missionaries, they turned and ran back into the bush, just as if angels or some other supernatural force were chasing them. In three hours, the chief, for whom this had been a legitimate power encounter, accepted Christ. Of 500 in the village, 300 became Christians. The village now has the largest Assemblies of God church in the Samoan Islands.

All words of knowledge won't produce that degree of drama, but since God is directly involved, all of them are awesome. My friend Omar Cabrera operates almost exclusively with words of knowledge in his healing ministry. In a rally of several thousand people, for example, God will tell him that he wants to heal people with hernias. So he calls those people forward, prays for them and then invites those who have been healed to give public testimony. Instead of hernias it may be cancer, kidney problems, addiction to tobacco, heart disease or what-have-you.

Once Omar Cabrera was negotiating with a group of hotel owners for some conference facilities he needed. One of them was in a four-legged walker, diagnosed with terminal cancer of the colon. Cabrera does not habitually pray for sick people he comes in casual contact with. But this time he received a word of knowledge that God wanted to heal the man. So when the deal was closed, he said, "I'm going to pray for you." He prayed and said, "Now, walk!" Much to his surprise, the man started walking on his own. Cabrera said, "Go home, God has healed you." In two weeks he attended one of Cabrera's rallies, ran up on the platform, and testified that not only had he been healed but that he also had been saved.

I do not recommend that you say to a person, "God has healed you," unless, like Cabrera, God Himself has revealed it directly to you. I rarely get this kind of a word, and even when it happens, I speak very tentatively, using all the subjunctives I can think of. In fact, I do not have the gift and I receive words of knowledge quite infrequently, but I do exercise my role and try to be open when God desires to speak directly to me.

To illustrate, in one of my two-week intensive church growth courses a missionary to Thailand, Joe Harbison, was enrolled. During the first week he asked prayer for guidance as to whether he should stay in school or go back to Thailand. After the class prayed, he felt that the Lord clearly had directed him to go back to Thailand for one year, then return to the School of World Mission. At our prayer time in the last day of class, he requested prayer for funds to return. I asked how much he still needed, and he said $1,000. I had called on Brad Brinson to be our prayer leader, and while Brad was praying for Joe Harbison's request, the Lord spoke to me with a precise word of knowledge: "Give $500; the rest is in this room." During the remainder of Brad's prayer I wrestled with the Lord about how I should tell the class, because I didn't want to show off any generosity that I might have in public. The right hand is not supposed to know what the left hand is doing. But God spoke again: "Say it!" So I obeyed.

When the prayer was over, I told the class that I felt God had told me to give the first half of the $1,000 and that the second half was supposed to be in the room. Instantly a Southern Baptist pastor, Dan Lindsey, raised his hand and said, "Here's the second half! God told me during the prayer that if someone offered the first half, I was to give the second half." Later Dan Lindsey said to me privately, "Nothing like this has ever happened to me before. It's not supposed to—I'm a Southern Baptist."

Scientific Investigation

One of the most fascinating parts of John Wimber's book *Power Healing,* is an appendix with a report from Dr. David C. Lewis of Nottingham University, England, with the long title, "Signs and Wonders in Sheffield: A Social Anthropologist's Analysis of Words of Knowledge, Manifestations of the Spirit, and the Effectiveness of Divine Healing." In 1985, Lewis investigated one of John Wimber's conferences, using "standard anthropological techniques of participant observation and in-depth interviews." The scientist argues that the words of knowledge announced publicly by the more experienced practitioners such as John Wimber and some of his associates can best be explained by their own hypothesis that they were speaking revelatory words from God. Such specific words as "a man in the balcony with a fungus on the bottom of the left foot which comes up between the last three toes to the top of the foot" can accurately be checked out, as Lewis did with many such words of knowledge. In order for any one of these to have happened by chance, Lewis calculates that instead of an audience of 3,000, which they had, they would have needed 750,000.[12]

For years, John Perkins, founder of the Voice of Calvary ministry in Mississippi and now leading the Harambee Center in Pasadena, California, has been a member of my 120 Fellowship Sunday School class. Back in November of 1983, a member of our prayer team, Cathryn Hoellwarth, received and announced a word of knowledge in class that God wanted to minister to someone who had a painful digestive disorder. She had a clear picture of the problem, but no one responded. So Cathryn prayed about it during the week, and on Thursday God told her that it was John Perkins. He had not been in class that Sunday.

But the next Sunday he was there. Cathryn approached him and asked if he had stomach problems, then began to describe the medical details with pinpoint accuracy. Perkins affirmed that her word was correct, that he had been suffering for months, that it was getting worse, and that this particular Sunday was his worst day yet. So Cathryn invited him to come to the prayer room after class.

This was back when we were all just getting used to third-wave type of phenomena. John Perkins, like many of us traditional evangelicals, had little background to prepare him for something like this, so he was hesitant. Words of knowledge can be scary at first. So he asked Doris and me if we would go to the prayer room with him, and we did. Tremendous power was evident, and we felt God had done something significant.

But we could not be sure, however, because just then Perkins was named to President Reagan's special Commission on Hunger and had to spend several weeks in other parts of the country. But when he returned to class in January, he stood up and said, "Now, I'm not an emotional man, but last November when the prayer team prayed for me after class, something happened to me. Since then I have felt better than I have in years."

Let's not get the idea that words of knowledge are essential for an effective healing ministry. Many who pray for the sick, myself included, see people healed with few or no words. But I think it is important to recognize this vehicle God frequently chooses to use. I am grateful for those around me who have the gift and who receive words of knowledge on a regular basis. And, although I do not have the gift, I want to keep myself open for God to give me occasional words when He chooses to do so.

Notes _____

1. *Emerging Trends*, Princeton Religious Research Center, June 1983, p. 4.
2. Cheryl Katz, "Religious Attitudes in Orange County Parallel Nationwide Findings," *Orange County Register*, Dec. 25, 1984, p. A16.
3. Robert L. Wise, "The Healing Ministry: What Is Really Involved?" *Christian Life*, June 1984, p. 51.
4. *Body Life*, newsletter of the 120 Fellowship, Lake Avenue Congregational Church, Pasadena, CA, Nov. 1987, p. 5.
5. Francis MacNutt, *The Power to Heal* (Notre Dame, IN: Ave Maria Press, 1977), p. 96.
6. John Gunstone, *Healing Power* (Ann Arbor, MI: Servant Books, 1987), p. 9.
7. Paul A. Cedar, "Ministering to the Sick on Sunday Morning," *Leadership 100*, Sept.-Oct. 1982, p. 17.
8. Lloyd John Ogilvie, *Why Not?* (Old Tappan, NJ: Fleming H. Revell Co., 1985), p. 39.
9. Oral Roberts, "How to Find Your Point of Contact," *Church Growth*, Seoul, Korea, Dec. 1983, p. 8.
10. For full details on the use of the five steps see John Wimber with Kevin Springer, *Power Healing* (San Francisco: Harper and Row, 1987), Chap. 11, 12. Another helpful summary is found in Ken Blue's *Authority to Heal* (Downers Grove, IL: InterVarsity Press, 1987), chap. 11.
11. Jack Hayford, "Healing for Today," *Charisma*, Sept. 1984, p. 43.
12. Wimber with Springer, *Power Healing*, pp. 248-269.

TEN

CRUCIAL QUESTIONS SURROUNDING A HEALING MINISTRY

When you start a healing ministry in your church, experience has shown that a standard set of questions is usually raised. Throughout this book I have tried to establish a framework for thinking about divine healing from the perspective of evangelical Christianity. While this perspective is intentionally non-Pentecostal and noncharismatic, it: (1) strongly affirms the work of God in these movements, (2) has learned and profited a great deal from them and (3) overlaps with them considerably in many areas. That framework, I trust, has given us biblical, theological and experiential or clinical bases to answer many of the questions ordinarily raised. I hope that those who have taken the pains to read and digest the material will have had many questions answered.

As I described in some detail in chapter 2, my own practical arena for exercising a ministry of healing has been the 120 Fellowship Sunday School class at Lake Avenue Congregational Church. For several years we have been praying for the sick within the structure of a traditional evangelical church, fortunately enough, without making the church sick. Across those years we have learned a great deal, and we have come to the place where we have been able to put down in writing our own philosophy of ministry relating to divine healing.

George Eckart, a Fuller Seminary graduate, has provided leadership through this process as the director of the class prayer/healing team. He wrote out the class philosophy of healing in a question and answer format, which is found in the appendix of this book. While I realize that each church needs to tailor-make its own philosophy of ministry to suit its particular needs, I do highly recommend George Eckart's document as a starting point, especially for traditional evangelical and mainline churches. Look it over, and if you find it helpful, use it.

Meanwhile, I have selected six of the crucial questions raised concerning healing ministries for this chapter. I have touched on some of them previously. Some appear on George Eckart's list and some don't. Each of these questions and others like them merit discussion in a whole chapter, however, I am only going to deal with them superficially. Nor is it my intention to be polemical and attempt to tear apart those with whom I might disagree. Different people whom I respect very highly answer the same questions in different ways, and I don't feel that much can be gained by proving them wrong so I can look right. That does not mean, however, that I do not believe that my point of view is the right one. If I thought it was wrong, I would change it immediately.

IS THE HEALING REAL?

Are the people we pray for really healed because we prayed? Can we prove a cause-and-effect relationship?

The answer to these questions takes us back to the issue of worldview. Believing is seeing. If you have already decided that God does not heal today, it will be impossible to prove to you that anyone has been healed through prayer. For example, today there are about 1500 members of the International Flat Earth Society, who firmly believe that the earth is flat, attributing the round earth theory to Satan. No amount of scientific proof that the earth is round has convinced them otherwise. By the same token, no quantity of medically documented cases of divine healing will convince those who have decided not to believe it is possible.

Rex Gardner deals with this issue quite extensively. He is a practicing physician who knows the medical profession well. As a Christian he asserts that God does heal directly through prayer. But as a physician he subjects himself to the behavioral norms of the medical profession and says that "even in well documented cases where patients and doctors are available for questioning and medical records can be examined, proof of miraculous cure is probably impossible."[1] This is sad but true. Because modern medicine is based on scientific rationalism, which, by definition, excludes divine intervention, we should not be surprised that since most doctors do not believe in the miraculous, they cannot see it.

Much ado is made by skeptics about the low number of officially verified miracles at Lourdes. But one of the top Lourdes experts, Father Rene Laurentin, agrees that it is again a matter of worldview. He found that some of the medical personnel on the Lourdes verification committees voted against verification "because they wanted one more test. And if they had gotten it, I think they would have asked for still another, without end." They operate on the postulate that everything in nature can be explained with reference to nature. Therefore, "rationalism in principle always has a way out."[2] As Jesus indicated, trying to prove the working of God to an unbelieving skeptic is a dead-end street.

I have a whole file of testimonies of medical doctors who confirm cases of divine healing. I used to try to collect more and ask for X-rays, naively thinking that if I could just produce enough of the really dramatic ones, I could convince everyone, including some theologians with whom I have been in dialogue. But I soon found that the only ones convinced, whether doctors or theologians, were those who already believed or those who were disposed to believe. Some skeptics, it might be noted, are open to examine evidence that might make them change their minds, like the apostle Thomas. Others have firmly made up their minds to remain unbelievers, and nothing will change them, like the Pharisees in Jesus' day. Trying to convince such unbelievers was, I discovered, no more productive than trying to convince Flat Earth Society members that the earth is round.

Aggressive skeptics frequently refer to William A. Nolen's book *Healing: A Doctor in Search of a Miracle.* In it Nolen, a physician, investigates several claims to healing, including Kathryn Kuhlman's ministries, and concludes that faith healers cannot cure organic diseases, only physicians can. I mention this in order to contrast Nolen's findings with those of Michael Cassidy.

In his book *Bursting the Wineskins*, Cassidy, the founder of African Enterprise, testifies that the turning point in his pilgrimage toward believing that God does actually use faith healers to cure organic diseases was a Kathryn Kuhlman meeting. He went, as he says, with a skeptical spirit and a "mood still set on sniffing out the phony." But he saw a seven-year-old boy with deformed legs who had never walked in his life take the braces off after prayer and run back and forth across the platform. Cassidy apparently was open enough to see things in Kathryn Kuhlman's ministry Nolen could not see. "That was how I came to believe that God still heals today," Cassidy says.[3]

Some scientifically designed research may come close to convincing some. For example, an article published in the proceedings of the American Heart Association describes the research of cardiologist Randolph C. Byrd of San Francisco General Hospital. He divided some 400 patients into two groups, then solicited prayer through home prayer groups for the patients in one group but not the other. None of the patients, nor other medical personnel, knew which group they were in. The group that was prayed for developed significantly fewer complications and fewer died.[4] How many physicians this will convince remains to be seen, because doctors frequently disagree with each other, to say nothing about their disagreement with other secular health professionals.

THE REAL QUESTION

As I see it, the question to be asked is not whether a given case of divine healing can be proven beyond all scientific doubt. The question is whether this account is backed by the type of evidence that indicates that accepting it as valid would be a reasonable response for one who assumes that such a thing is possible.

If this is the case, and I believe it is, why not accept testimonies, just like we do for personal salvation? The most generally acceptable way of verifying conversions is through testimonies. For example, I was a drunk before I was saved, and God changed my life through the new birth. How much more verification do you need to really believe me? Should I get some social worker's report? Should I be psychoanalyzed? Should I take a lie detector test? Can I produce scientific proof that I have been born again? How do I know my pastor is really saved? Or my wife? Yes, we expect to see the fruits of repentance in the life, but in medical cases we also expect to see symptoms relieved. Suppose an otherwise reasonable person tells me that their teeth were decayed, that someone prayed for them, and that God filled the teeth directly? I look, and sure enough, the teeth are filled. Do I really need dental charts? When the skeptics questioned the blind man that Jesus healed, he responded, "One thing I know: that though I was blind, now I see" (John 9:25). It was an appropriate answer then, and it is now.

My current position is that unless I have special reason not to believe it (such as the testimony of an African woman who said she had been pregnant for six years and God delivered twins through prayer), I take the testimonies of sincere, lucid people at face value. I don't want to be gullible, but I do want to model the attitude advocated by the apostle Paul: love "believes all things" (1 Cor. 13:7). When there is a choice, I think it is better to be a believer than a skeptic. I would rather follow Jesus' rule than Thomas' rule. Jesus said of Thomas the skeptic, "Thomas, because you have seen Me, you have believed." Jesus' rule is "Blessed are those who have not seen and yet have believed" (John 20:29).

Accountability

Nevertheless, I believe in accountability. I am scientific enough to want to check on my own effectiveness. I pray for the sick, but am I successful? How many should be

Groups or churches that have gained a public reputation for a faith healing ministry would do well to keep track of their results and share this information publicly.

healed in order to call a healing ministry successful? Jesus was probably looking at 100 percent. Before I became part of the third wave, I was looking at something more like zero percent. So possibly I should be interested in how much higher than zero my percentage is, rather than how much lower than 100 percent. Regardless of the point of comparison, I do take pains to give a report form to each person I pray for. It is in a self-addressed return envelope, and I ask them to send it back when enough time elapses for them to know whether something has happened or not. It has places to check for no improvement, some improvement, considerable improvement and completely well. Several other questions fill in background data.

I began this process in the fall of 1986. For the years 1986 and 1987, I have received 114 forms. The tally runs as follows:

No improvement	18%
Some improvement	28%
Considerable improvement	25%
Completely well	29%

Whether this could be labeled successful or not, I don't know, but it is encouraging. Of course, I do not know the percentages of unreturned forms. But of those returned, to know that 82 percent of those I prayed for feel better afterwards is heartening. And 29 percent completely well? I'm awfully glad I prayed, and so are they. My hope is that the 29 percent will be higher each year as I go along.

In my opinion, individuals, groups or churches that have gained a public reputation for a faith healing ministry would do well to keep track of their results and share this information publicly. One of the best organized and most pastorally responsible healing ministries I know of is the Small Ministry Teams soaking prayer service of Vineyard Christian Fellowship of Anaheim, California. Bill McReynolds, one of John Wimber's associate pastors, supervises no fewer than 325 trained laypeople who form 80 prayer teams. Under strictly supervised clinical conditions a team contracts with an individual for six weekly one-hour prayer therapy sessions.

In 1987 they ministered to over 600 people with the following results:

No improvement	19%
Some or considerable improvement	58%
Completely well	26%

I find it remarkable that Vineyard's and my percentage would turn out to be virtually identical. How they would compare with the results of medical doctors or psychiatrists I do not know since such records are rarely made public.

Can Healing Be Counterfeited?

The world has its share of phonies. Even in the days of Jesus there were people prophesying and casting out demons and doing miracles in Jesus' name, but He said He didn't even know them (see Matt. 7:22,23). Paul warns Timothy of deceiving spirits and doctrines of demons (see 1 Tim. 4:1). In the book of Revelation we read of the beast performing great signs (see 13:13-14) and spirits of demons performing signs (see 16:14) and the false prophet working signs (see 19:20). Obviously there is supernatural power out there that is not of God.

This power is used to counterfeit the true miracles of God. Timothy Warner says, "These counterfeit miracles range all the way from false fruits and gifts of the Spirit to healings and other more dramatic things."[5] We see counterfeits in Haitian voodoo, in Brazilian spiritism, in African traditional religions, in the occult here in the U.S. and wherever witchcraft, magic and astrology are present. In Thailand, three-year-old "Dr. Noi" heals thousands with a magical tree bark. In India Hindus pierce their bodies with hooks and walk barefoot on live coals, feeling no pain.

This power of Satan at times is pitted against the power of God. This was the case as Moses was leading the people of Israel out of Egypt. It was only after a massive power encounter that Pharaoh would finally let God's people go. His magicians were able to produce miraculous counterfeits—but only to a point. They really looked pretty bad. They lost the warm-up when Aaron's rod consumed the rods of the magicians. They did duplicate the first two plagues of turning the river into blood and frogs. But then they ran out of power and could not match the other eight. God won that encounter quite decisively, but the magicians had proved they could do some counterfeiting, drawing on the power of the enemy (see Exod. 7:11,22; 8:7).

Even supposed Christians get into counterfeiting. Jim Jones would fake cancer cures by pulling chicken livers and other organs from the throats of those he prayed for. Peter Popoff received "words of knowledge" in his healing services, which turned out to be messages from his wife transmitted on a high-tech electronic device. No wonder Dave Hunt became disturbed and wrote his best-selling *The Seduction of Christianity*. Unfortunately, while raising good questions, Hunt tends to go to extremes with his answers, labeling as seducers not just the Jim Joneses and Peter Popoffs but also the John Wimbers and the Robert Wises and the Richard Fosters and the Paul Yonggi Chos. I agree with Richard Lovelace who affirms that the Body of Christ does need an alarm system in the form of critics who, like white corpuscles, identify and attack germs. "But," says Lovelace, "an overactive immune system will reject needed parts in the body, as often happens in organ transplants, because it has wrongly identified these as hostile."[6]

How To Tell the Difference

How, then, can we tell the difference between the true and the counterfeit? I believe there are three ways.

First, we use sanctified common sense. The Bible describes mature Christians as "those who by reason of use have their senses exercised to discern both good and evil" (Heb. 5:14). As we get to know Jesus Christ better, we become more sensitive to what is not of God. For example, an advertisement in *Globe* says, "I am Andreika and I can change the course of destiny. Pay me and I shall cast a spell in your favor." The price? $13.50. Christian common sense will tell us that this is rooted in evil, not in good, even though it goes on to promise health and happiness.

Second, we use the gift of discernment. In 1 Corinthians 12:10 we find "discerning of spirits" in one of the major lists of spiritual gifts. My understanding is that this is the special ability that God gives to certain members of the Body of Christ to know with assurance whether certain behavior purported to be of God is in reality divine, human or satanic.[7] Although I do not have the gift myself, many of my friends do. Michael Green, for instance, says, "I find that, quite unsought by me, I possess this gift, and it is very useful in difficult pastoral situations."[8] Some members of my 120 Fellowship Sunday School class have it as well, and I call on them when special discernment is needed.

Third, we look for the fruit of the Spirit. What are the end results of the healings or miracles? James gives us some good hints as to how to tell the "wisdom that is from above" from wisdom that is "earthly, sensual, demonic." Satan's wisdom produces fruits of envy, self-seeking, boasting, and lying. God's is "peaceable, gentle, willing to yield, full of mercy and good fruits, without partiality and without hypocrisy" (Jas. 3:17). Michael Harper points out that "Christianity is alone amongst the world's religions in claiming to possess by the grace of God and the power of the Holy Spirit the ability to heal the sick and do miracles."[9]

I like the way Barton Stone, that great leader of the Churches of Christ movement of the last century, evaluated some revival phenomena that were new to him and that he did not understand. After investigating what had happened, he admitted that the devil always tries to ape the works of God and bring them into disrepute. But the phenomena he saw "cannot be a satanic work," because they "bring men to a humble confession and forsaking of sin—to solemn prayer-fervent praise and thanksgiving, and to sincere and affectionate exhortations to sinners to repent and go to Jesus the Saviour."[10]

Those are good indicators. So is Paul Hiebert's list. As guides for discerning the manifestations of God's Spirit over against those of the enemy, Hiebert lists the glory of God, the lordship of Christ, agreement with the Scriptures, the fruit of the Spirit, spiritual maturity, the balance of presenting the whole gospel, the unity of the Body of Christ and wholism.[11] This is a checklist I find very useful in the ongoing task of recognizing the true and the counterfeit.

Let's not fall into the trap of overreacting to the knowledge that Satan can and does counterfeit God's works. Let's not forsake the power on those grounds. Timothy Warner says this would be "like refusing to spend a twenty-dollar bill because you've heard that there are counterfeit twenties in circulation."[12]

DO WE MANIPULATE GOD?

The essence of magic is that the practitioner, whether a shaman, medium, witch, channeler, high priest, sorcerer or what-have-you, exercises power to manipulate supernatural forces to do whatever they ask. Through magical powers they can cause people to die, get sick, get well, attract another sexually, find a mate or break up a marriage, lose their crops, win fights, and any number of other things.

This is not the Christian way. Christianity and magic

are as incompatible as the positive poles of two magnets. That is why, when we begin a healing ministry in our churches, we must be conscious of the ever-present

When we begin a healing ministry in our churches, we must be conscious of the ever-present danger of practicing magic with a Christian veneer.

danger of practicing magic with a Christian veneer. The danger should not keep us from a powerful ministry of the miraculous, however, and it need not if we keep two important basic principles in mind each time: (1) We must avoid manipulation, and (2) we must avoid capitulation.

First, we must avoid manipulating God. This is not easy to do, because He is our Father. Those of us who have reared children know the inborn tendency of children to try to manipulate their parents. But as parents we usually take it in stride and find that it doesn't destroy our basic love relationship with one another. Sometimes we even let our children get away with it, but not too often. I think God also takes our inborn manipulating tendencies in stride, and He has His ways of letting us know when we're overdoing it.

FIVE GUIDELINES

Still, we do well to take all the conscious steps we can to avoid even the appearance that we are performing magic. I have touched on several of these in previous chapters, but here are five guidelines that will help us avoid manipulation:

1. Do not attempt to give orders to God or to write His script for Him. When I first began praying for the sick, I used to develop mental scenarios of this celebrity or that one getting healed and turning the world upside down for Jesus. It was like saying, "Hey, God. I've got a fantastic idea for you. Have you ever thought of this one?" I quickly learned that He wasn't interested.

2. Do not use formulas or techniques for healing. I realize that some more liturgical groups have written out healing liturgies and healing prayers, and they are often very effective. But let's not fall into the trap of thinking that what makes the healing take place is saying the right words, creating the right emotional climate, being in the right environment, naming and claiming it correctly, using the right oil or holding our hands in the right way when we pray. All of the above might be helpful at times, but none produces healing. Even the name of Jesus itself is not an effective formula per se, as the seven sons of Sceva quickly found out (see Acts 19:13-16).

3. Always seek God's will for the healing. John says that God will hear our prayers "if we ask anything according to His will" (1 John 5:14).

4. Follow Jesus' example in being an open channel for the Father to do what He wants to do through you. Chapter 5 elaborates on this guideline.

5. Do not attribute the results of prayer for the sick, whether positive or negative, to the faith level or the attitude of the sick person. I will expand on this later.

CAPITULATING TO THE STATUS QUO

The second major principle for dealing with magic is to

avoid capitulation to the status quo. Some have developed an unfortunate type of magic-phobia that has virtually paralyzed them and is an obstacle to an effective healing ministry. Here are five other guidelines to help keep the pendulum from swinging too far in the opposite direction:

1. Make your petitions known to the Father. We are invited to do this time and again in the Scripture. We boldly pray, "Give us this day our daily bread." This is not considered manipulation.

2. Petition the Father in the name of Jesus. While the seven sons of Sceva used Jesus' name in vain, we use it properly. "If you ask anything in My name, I will do it" (John 14:14).

3. Use material substances such as oil when you feel led. James recommends anointing with oil (see 5:14). The disciples healed many by anointing them with oil (see Mark 6:13).

4. Welcome healing through liturgical forms including baptism and holy communion. My good friend Fred Luthy was once called to the hospital essentially to administer the last rites to a woman who was dying of emphysema and in a coma. The doctors had given her up, and the family had been called in. She was not baptized, and the family knew this was something she wanted, so Fred felt led to baptize her that night. The next day she came to, sat up in bed bright-eyed, and motioned for a pad of paper to write on because her mouth and throat were full of tubes and she couldn't talk. Her note came right to the point: "I'm hungry!"

5. Accept and exercise the authority that God gives you to heal the sick and cast out demons. Jesus told the 70 to "heal the sick who are there" (Luke 10:9).

Although we know that ultimately only God heals, the Scripture does not hesitate at times to say things like "Stephen, full of faith and power, did great wonders and signs among the people" (Acts 6:8). This is not considered to reflect the use of a Christian magic.

HOW MUCH FAITH IS NEEDED?

While God at times performs miraculous works sovereignly and directly as He did with Saul on the Damascus Road, that is the exception. The rule that we find both in the Bible and in practical experience is that He ordinarily uses human agents. And an essential part of the connection for the power of God to flow through human agents is faith. But the role that faith plays is often misunderstood. We need to be clear in two important areas: the agent of faith and the amount of faith.

The agent of faith raises the question: Who needs faith for the healing to take place? The Bible gives us separate illustrations of the agent of faith being the sick person, intermediaries and the healer.

The faith of the sick is sometimes connected to the healing. Two blind men came up to Jesus for healing. He said, "Do you believe that I am able to do this?" When they said yes, Jesus responded, "According to your faith let it be to you." And they both were healed (see Matt. 9:27-31).

But this is not always the case. The centurion's servant was healed of paralysis without even knowing Jesus was healing him, so far as we are informed. In this case an intermediary, the centurion, had the faith. Jesus said, "I have not found such great faith, not even in Israel!" (8:10).

When Peter and John approached the lame man at the Temple gate, he didn't even expect to be healed, nor were there any intermediaries. Peter was the agent of faith in this case when he said, "Silver and gold I do not have, but what I do have I give you: In the name of Jesus Christ of Nazareth, rise up and walk" (Acts 3:6).

Illustrations for each one of these three categories could be multiplied, but the point has been made. In different cases God will use different agents of faith. One of the most common errors made in this regard is to say to a sick person who is not healed through prayer, "If you only had enough faith, you would get well." That is not only unbiblical, it is also inhumane, because it adds unnecessary pain to the affliction they already have.

The amount of faith is the second area. How much faith does it take to make the healing happen? The answer to this is that there is no answer. The more faith the better, of course. Stephen did many miracles because he was "full of faith and power" (Acts 6:8). But there are numerous cases of others having faith only the size of a mustard seed and seeing remarkable things happen. I previously mentioned how little faith I had when I saw ears grow on the head of a boy born without ears.

I like the story that Kate Semmerling tells of her experience as a student nurse in a clinic in Haiti. A woman brought a small boy with crippled legs. He could not stand or walk. She tried to explain that there was nothing she could do, but she wanted to get rid of the woman so, as she says, "I sighed and offered to pray for her—a God-bless-this-woman-type of prayer that would send her on her way." But there was a grain of faith that told her God could heal, although she expected nothing. She put her hands on the crippled legs and said, "Dear

God, please come and do your work here."
    That was enough faith in that case. Over the next five
minutes the legs pumped up as if they were small bal-
loons, and they filled with new muscle. Kate said, "I
thought I was in the Twilight Zone. I had never seen anything like this happen before." The boy's legs became
normal, and he stood up and walked around. Kate's
response: "Oh my God, look at this!"[13] Not a strong indication of faith.

CAN SUFFERING BE BENEFICIAL?

Suffering is an extremely complex issue, both biblically
and theologically. It raises questions that really need not
only a chapter but a whole book to address. Many books
have been written on it, and many more will be written.
Recognizing this, I have elected in this brief section to
look at some of the issues that most directly relate to our
ministry as we pray for the sick.
    One of these is commonly referred to as redemptive
suffering. The idea behind it is that suffering is beneficial, and through it our relationship to God will be
enhanced.
    No one has said it better than Ken Blue. He feels that
the "notion that sickness is essentially good for us" and
that "it is sent to us to purify the soul and build character" constitutes one of the greatest hindrances to effective healing ministries today. Because of this idea, many
believe it is more Christlike to endure illnesses than to
be healed. In fact, seeking healing is considered to be
selfish.[14] Some say that if we ask God to heal us, we display our captivity to a culture of entitlements.
    Francis MacNutt adds, "When we say God sends

sickness or asks us to endure it, we are creating for many people an image of God they must eventually reject. What human mother or father would choose cancer for their daughter in order to tame her pride?"[15] Mac-Nutt selects Latin America to illustrate where such teaching can lead. He says that because "God is somehow portrayed as mysteriously desiring man to suffer in a redemptive way," many Latin Americans feel that when sickness comes, it is God's will. So in order to regain health, they obviously would not go to God but to a witch doctor. This, MacNutt argues, is a tragic theological reversal. "The people treat God as if he were a pagan deity to be appeased by suffering. But for healing, they turn to the world of spirits and demons."[16]

None of this is to say that there cannot be benefit in suffering. I stressed this in chapter 4. There I mentioned how Paul ultimately benefited from his "thorn in the flesh" (see 2 Cor. 12:7-10). Some suffering is redemptive. James tells us to "count it all joy when you fall into various trials" (1:2), because testing produces patience and patience helps mature us. Hebrews says that chastening from the Father produces "the peaceable fruit of righteousness" (12:11). But while this is part of the total picture, God is more often seen biblically as a deliverer from suffering rather than a producer of suffering.

ILLNESS AND SUFFERING

It is helpful not to confuse illness in particular with suffering in general. With rare exceptions, the New Testament references to suffering relate to demonic attacks, persecution for the sake of the gospel or divine judgment, not to human illness. An informative study of this was done by Peter H. Davids. He found that in the *afflic-tion* word group (Greek, *thlipsis*), 54 appearances in the New Testament refer to persecution, oppression, famine or eschatological judgment. The only other one refers to labor pains (see John 16:21). The *suffer* word group (Greek, *pascho*) appears 65 times. Only one of them relates to illness, and that one is specifically attributed to a demonic attack (see Matt. 17:15). In another, interest-ingly enough, the sick woman's suffering does not apply to her illness but to the treatment she received from the physicians (Mark 5:26).[17]

The appropriate Christian responses to suffering on one hand and illness on the other are suggested in James 5:13-15. "Is anyone among you suffering?" Response: "Let him pray." Then, "Is anyone among you sick?" Response: "Let him call for the elders of the church, and let them pray over him . . . and the Lord will raise him up."

It is curious that those who stress the redemptive benefits of sickness rather than the desire to ask God to heal them seem to be inconsistent when they or their loved ones get sick. I like A. B. Simpson's response: "Well, if those who urge and claim to practice this sug-gestion would really accept their sickness, and lie pas-sive under it, they would at least be consistent. But do they not send for a doctor, and do their best to get out of this 'sweet will of God'?"[18] Of course they do. What theo-logian or ethicist would advise their spouse who has a severe toothache to stay home and seek redemptive benefit rather than go to the dentist? It turns out in prac-tice that the root of the problem is not whether sickness should be healed, but who should heal it. It's okay for doctors or dentists to do it, but it seems presumptuous to ask God to do it directly.

WHY ARE SOME NOT HEALED?

It is a fact of life that some Christians follow the instructions of James 5 to the letter and have the elders anoint them with oil and pray and they also seek the best medical treatment available, and yet they remain sick. Joni Eareckson Tada is one of the best known living examples. With no lack of faith on her part, the part of intermediaries or on the part of those who have laid on hands and anointed her with oil, she remains a quadriplegic in her wheelchair.

Why?

When I addressed the life-style of the kingdom in chapter 4, I said that nobody really knows the answer to that one, and if someone finds it, they should receive a Nobel prize in theology. But perhaps no one needs that prize. Perhaps Robert Wise is correct when he advises us not even to ask why, because "Knowing that God stands with me means that I really don't have to have an answer for the all-mysterious 'whys' of my life." He suggests that we trade the why question in for a better one: What? What does this mean for me, and how can God use my situation?[19]

I face this all the time. Although a large percentage were improved to one degree or another, nevertheless 71 percent of the people I have prayed for over the last two years are still sick to some degree after the prayer is over. Only 29 percent are completely healed. I don't think this is strange, but I don't have the comparative percentages on others who also have a gift or ministry of healing to check it out. I have heard John Wimber say on occasion, "More people I pray for are not healed than are." But, as I have mentioned previously, virtually everyone who receives healing prayer is helped one way or another. In the final analysis, to cite Charles Kraft, ministry is even more important than healing.

WAITING FOR THE MIRACLE

In George Eckart's appendix, you will see a question: What pastoral care is given those who do not receive healing? He says that the desire of his team is "to mirror the love, concern, grace and commitment of the Lord Jesus to such a degree that the context of ministry is therapeutic even if the specific request remains, as yet, unanswered." Notice the phrase *as yet*. Timing is important, and those we pray for need to know that the miracle might still come.

I learned this when, three years ago, John Wimber prayed against the bursitis I had been suffering from in both shoulders. For three years I could not lift my elbows as high as my shoulders. When he prayed, however, nothing happened. But a woman there received a word of knowledge that I was to stretch my shoulders to the point where they hurt and a little more each day. I did, and in three weeks it was completely gone and has been ever since.

Robert Wise recommends that while you are waiting for a miracle, try to assume a neutral position with one foot in the expectation that it will happen and with the other in the possibility that it won't. He says, "Don't hesitate to look yourself in the eye" and face your fears, angers and apprehensions.[20] He then adds three practical pieces of advice: First, don't practice wishful thinking. Don't be like the child who prays that God will change the spinach into ice cream. Second, don't try to psych yourself out. Your healing does not depend on your frame of mind. And, third, don't make bargains with God. If you do, you're back to the magic we spoke about earlier.[21]

How long do we wait for the miracle to happen? Well, God promised Abraham and Sarah a child, and they had to wait 25 years for it to happen. They made a few mistakes they would not want to repeat while they were waiting. The apostle Paul prayed three times that his thorn in the flesh would be taken away. Then he didn't pray anymore, but accepted it. Why did he stop? Because God said to him, "My grace is sufficient for you" (2 Cor. 12:9). My recommendation to people who are not immediately healed is that they continue to ask for prayer, whether 3 times or 33 times, until God tells them to stop, as He did the apostle Paul.

I do not know of anyone or any group involved in healing ministries who would not like to see their effectiveness improved. Some, like Francis MacNutt, have identified specific reasons why some people are not healed. He lists lack of faith, redemptive suffering, a false value attached to suffering, sin, not praying specifically, faulty diagnosis, refusal to see medicine as a way God heals, not using the natural means of preserving health, timing, a different person is to be the instrument of healing and a social environment that prevents healing from taking place.[22] I could join him in giving illustrations from my own ministry for each of his points.

If we follow the suggestion of turning the why question into a what question, we are on the right track, pastorally speaking. Joni Eareckson Tada has led the way in coming to terms with the fact that "Christ, who is always compassionate, just, pure, and holy, has and always will deal with His children in varied, individual and always changing ways. He stays the same, but His dealings with men and women are always changing. Just because He healed at one time does not mean He is bound to heal every time." So when she became confined to a wheelchair and faced the question: "Was I going to idle my time away or use whatever I had left for God's glory?" She made a good choice and decided to go for it for God.[23]

Few have reflected more than Joni about the question we are discussing: Why are some not healed? Her conclusion is sensitive and well-reasoned. She first affirms, "God certainly can, and sometimes does, heal people in a miraculous way today." She then adds, "But the Bible does not teach that He will always heal those who come to Him in faith. He sovereignly reserves the right to heal or not to heal as He sees fit."[24]

Joni also lives in the hope of heaven when she will be welcomed home and she will have a new body. "I myself will be able to run to friends and embrace them for the first time," she says. "I will lift my new hands before the hierarchy of heaven—shouting to everyone within earshot, 'Worthy is the Lamb who was slain to receive blessing and honor. For He freed my soul from the clutches of sin and death, and now He has freed my body as well!'"[25]

This is Joni's hope, and mine, and that of every Christian I know. It is a major reason why, while there is still time, nothing could be more important in this life than sharing the saving gospel of Jesus Christ with those who are yet to believe. As Jesus told His disciples, our greatest rejoicing should come knowing that our names are written in heaven (see Luke 10:20). We *may* be healed now; we *shall* be healed then.

Notes ————————————————————————————

1. Rex Gardner, "Miracles of Healing in Anglo-Celtic Northumbria as Recorded by the Venerable Bede and His Contemporaries: A Reappraisal in the Light of Twentieth Century Experience," *British Medical Journal*, Dec. 1983, p. 6. See also Gardner's *Healing Miracles* (London: Darton, Longman and Todd, 1986), chap. 1 and 2.

2. Rene Laurentin, *Miracles in El Paso?* (Ann Arbor, MI: Servant Books, 1982), p. 91.

3. Michael Cassidy, *Bursting the Wineskins* (Wheaton, IL: Harold Shaw Publishers, 1983), pp. 43-45. Interestingly enough, Michael Harper's spiritual pilgrimage toward a healing ministry was also greatly helped in a Kathryn Kuhlman meeting when he saw a young man healed of emphysema. See *The Healings of Jesus* (Downers Grove, IL: InterVarsity Press, 1986), pp. 13,14.

4. Byrd, Randolph C., "Positive Therapeutic Effects of Intercessory Prayer in a Coronary Care Unit Population," *Circulation*, Part II, Vol. 70, No. 4, Oct. 1984, Abstract No. 845, p. II-212. The Abstract reads as follows:

    Intercessory prayer (IP), one of the oldest forms of therapy, has had little attention in the medical literature. To evaluate the effects of IP in a coronary care unit (CCU) population, a randomized double blind protocol was followed. Over a 10-month period, 393 CCU admissions were randomized, after signing informed consent, to an intercessory prayer group (IPG), 192 patients (pts), or to a no prayer group (NPG), 201 pts. The IPG, while hospitalized, received IP by participating Christians praying outside the hospital; the NPG did not. On entry into the study there was no statistical difference between the groups on any of the 34 variables. Logistic analysis failed to separate the groups on the entry variables. After entry, the IPG had statistically less pulmonary edema, 6 pts vs 18 pts (p ÷ 0.03); was intubated less frequently, none vs 12 pts (p ÷ 0.002), and received less antibiotics, 3 pts vs 16 pts (p ÷ 0.007). In conclusion, IP appears to have a beneficial effect in pts in a CCU.

5. Timothy M. Warner, "A Response to Wagner," *Trinity World Forum*, Spring 1986, p. 5.

6. Richard Lovelace, "Countering the Devil's Tactics," *Charisma*, Dec. 1984, p. 10.

7. C. Peter Wagner, *Your Spiritual Gifts Can Help Your Church Grow* (Ventura, CA: Regal Books, Div. of Gospel Light Publications, 1979), p. 261.

8. Michael Green, *I Believe in Satan's Downfall* (Grand Rapids, MI: Wm. B. Eerdmans Pub. Co., 1981), p. 133.

9. Harper, *Healings*, p. 130.

10. Cited in Vinson Synan, *The Twentieth-Century Pentecostal Explosion* (Altamonte Springs, FL: Creation House, 1987), p. 57.

11. Paul G. Hiebert, "Discerning the Work of God," *Charismatic Experiences in History*, Cecil M. Robeck, Jr., ed. (Peabody, MA: Henderson, 1985), pp. 151-159.

12. Warner, "A Response to Wagner," p. 5.
13. Kate Semmerling with Andres Tapia, "Haiti," *U* magazine, Feb. 1987, p. 13.
14. Ken Blue, *Authority to Heal* (Downers Grove, IL: InterVarsity Press, 1987), pp. 21-22.
15. Francis MacNutt, *The Power to Heal* (Notre Dame, IN: Ave Maria Press, 1977), p. 139.
16. Francis MacNutt, *Healing* (Notre Dame, IN: Ave Maria Press, 1974), pp. 106-107.
17. Peter H. Davids, "Suffering: Endurance and Relief," *First Fruits*, July/Aug. 1986, pp. 8,9.
18. A. B. Simpson, *The Gospel of Healing* (Harrisburg, PA: Christian Publications, 1915 rev.), pp. 57,58.
19. Robert L. Wise, *When There Is No Miracle* (Ventura, CA: Regal Books, Div. of Gospel Light Publications, 1977), p. 99.
20. Ibid., p. 151.
21. Ibid., p. 153.
22. MacNutt, *Healing*, pp. 249-260.
23. Joni Eareckson Tada, "His Strength Made Perfect," *Christian Life*, July 1986, pp. 17,18.
24. Joni Eareckson Tada and Steve Estes, *A Step Further* (Grand Rapids, MI: Zondervan Publishing House, 1978), p. 127.
25. Ibid., pp. 184,185.

APPENDIX

Common Questions Concerning the
Ministry of Healing in The 120 Fellowship of
Lake Avenue Congregational Church
Pasadena, California

George W. Eckart

How do you understand sickness?

We believe that sickness is the physical or emotional dysfunction of an individual. Specific instances of illness can be caused by any one or a combination of organic, psychological or spiritual disorders or injuries. We believe that an effective healing ministry needs to have a comprehensive perspective of the causes of sickness and its treatment.

Should the Church of Jesus Christ have a ministry of healing today?

Yes! We believe the Church of Jesus Christ is to exercise a ministry of healing today. The gifts of healing have never been withdrawn from the Church. Therefore, along with our best efforts at encouraging proper medical care, expectant prayer on behalf of the sick should also be an important component in the Church's ministry to those in need.

How does the ministry of healing relate to the other ministries of the Church?

We believe that preaching the gospel to the lost, healing the sick, casting out demons, caring for the poor and the pursuit of justice are all facets of the ministry the Lord Jesus Christ has passed on to His Church. We believe that each evidences the in-breaking of the powers of the kingdom to a fallen world in need of redemption in every sphere.

Can any Christian pray for the sick and expect the sick to be made well?

Yes! We believe that any Christian can pray for the sick and at least some of the time see the sick made well.

According to the apostle Paul, not every Christian has the same spiritual gift. If every Christian does not have a gift of healing, how then can any Christian pray for the sick and expect the sick to be made well?

Not every Christian has a gift of healing. However, we do not believe that one needs a gift of healing in order to see the sick made well. We distinguish between gifts and roles. We believe that every spiritual gift has a corresponding role. Just as one does not need the gift of evangelism in order to lead someone to Christ, so we believe that one does not need a gift of healing in order to effectively pray for the sick. The one who ministers in a gift will be consistently more effective in the specific area of service than the one who ministers out of their role as a Christian. Yet, we believe that either the one who has a gift of healing or the one who simply prays out of their role as a Christian can be effective in seeing the sick made well.

Is it necessary for someone to speak in tongues in order to be effective in praying for the sick?

No! While we believe that tongues is a contemporary gift of the Holy Spirit, we do not recognize it as the initial evidence of the so-called "baptism of the Holy Spirit," nor do we believe that speaking in tongues is essential in order to be effective in praying for the sick.

Does God always heal the sick when we ask Him to do so?

We do not believe that the Lord always heals every time we ask Him to do so. Nor do we believe that the Bible leads us to expect Him to send healing every time we ask. Scripture affirms that in the Age to Come the Lord will do away with every tear from our eyes. All healing will be complete and permanent. "There shall be no more death, nor sorrow, nor crying; and there shall be no more pain, for the former things have passed away." (Rev. 21:4). While we have tasted of the powers of the Age to Come, the full realization of the blessings of the Age to Come belong to the future. We are assured of complete and final healing only then but not now.

Where does the power to heal reside?

The power to heal resides with God alone. Jesus did only what the Father was doing (see John 5:19-21), and said only what the Father gave Him to say (see 12:49,50). As a result, there was blessing and benefit in His deeds and words. Like Jesus, we believe our responsibility is to cultivate an intimate dependence upon the Holy Spirit so as to be ready to walk in the good works which God "prepared beforehand." All we can do is pray. It is the Lord's responsibility to heal.

What does it mean to have "faith for healing"?

By "faith" we mean a willingness to come before Jesus and expectantly ask for His healing touch while releasing ourselves into His loving care trusting Him to do what is best for us. We do not believe that faith is a tool for coercing God to heal. Nor is it a level of credulity heightened by excessive emotionalism which seeks to deny the reality of symptoms.

What is the relationship between healing and faith?

Generally, we believe that faith needs to be present for healing to take place (see Mark 6:1-6). Ideally, faith should be present in the one asking for prayer. However, we believe, that "healing faith" could also be effectively present in the one praying or in the community that surrounds the ministry.

Should Christians "claim" their healing and disregard symptoms that might persist following prayer?

While it is possible that the Lord may occasionally direct an individual to "claim" healing prior to actually receiving it, this is not the "obedience of faith" we encourage among those asking for prayer. The Lord Jesus never asked anyone to "claim" their healing during His own earthly ministry. Therefore, we believe it is unwise to make a practice out of doing so in ours.

Should someone who has received prayer for healing stop taking prescribed medicine as a step of faith?

A medical doctor is the only one who has the authority to remove a patient from a prescribed medication. Those who believe they have received healing for a condition requiring medication should check with their doctor before altering their prescribed treatment.

Should a person who has received prayer for healing also seek the services of a physician or does doing so evidence a lack of faith?

We believe that modern medicine (including psychotherapy) is one of the means the Lord uses to minister healing to those in need. We do not believe that seeking prayer for healing and seeking the care of a medical professional are mutually exclusive or contradictory events. On occasion, Jesus referred to Himself as a physician (see Mark 2:17) and seemed to be favorably inclined toward the service they provide (see Matt. 9:12).

Why is it that you do not conduct "healing services" but

prefer to pray with individuals privately using small ministry teams?

We prefer small ministry teams to large "healing services" for three reasons:

1. A small ministry team affords a more confidential environment where the privacy of individuals requesting prayer can be more easily maintained.

2. Small ministry teams are generally better adapted to encourage in-depth ministry within the context of caring personal relationships.

3. A small ministry team has at its disposal a greater variety of spiritual gifts and experiences than is generally present in any one individual alone.

Is most healing instantaneous or does it occur over a period of time?

In Jesus' ministry, most healing appears to have been instantaneous. There were occasions, however, in which healing seemed to occur over a period of time (see Mark 8:22-26; 5:8). In our ministry, most healing seems to occur over a period of time yet, on many occasions, healing is instantaneous.

Is all sickness the specific result of demonic infestation?

No! While Scripture indicates that sickness can result from demonic influence (see Luke 13:11; Matt. 8:28), we believe that it is incorrect to consider all or most physi-

cal or mental dysfunction as demonic in origin. "Possession," the most extreme form of demonization, may
occur today but its instance is extremely rare. In all
cases, however, Christians are more than conquerors
through Christ Jesus our Lord (see Rom. 8:37).

What pastoral care is given to those who do not receive healing?

There seems to be a divine timing both in salvation and
in healing. As a result, we encourage those who do not
receive healing to let us pray for them again at another
time. It is important to us to make sure that those who
have yet to receive healing are not weighted down with a
sense of failure or guilt. As a ministry team, our aim is to
mirror the love, concern, grace and commitment of the
Lord Jesus to such a degree that the context of ministry
is therapeutic even if the specific request remains, as
yet, unanswered.

Can sickness be used by God for His glory?

Yes! Although sickness is not God's perfect will for our
life, we believe that suffering and trials of any kind,
including persistent sickness, can be used by God to
perfect our faith and to bring glory to His name (1 Pet.
1:6,7).

Index